Copyright 2008 by Janice Brantle
Library of Congress Cataloging-In-Publication Data
Brantle, Janice
From the Brink of Insanity Comes the Light/Janice Brantle
ISBN: 9781435760417

This book is dedicated to the women in my family: Joanie for showing me faith, Kim for showing me dedication, Leslie for showing me God is real, Margaret for showing me perseverance, and My Mom Theresa for showing us all how to survive in this crazy, mixed up world.

Prologue

Where am I? I look around and nothing is familiar. The noise is unbearable. Or is that in my head? "Beep!" The blare of a car horn jolts me back to reality. Heading nowhere in particular, I have been walking around in the cold and dark of night. I have to clear my head. These damn tears just won't stop flowing. Snowing. Pretty. . Why God, why? It is so cold out here. How did I get here and what happened to my coat? I can't see past these damn tears. What's all this red, stickiness on my hands? Those lights are bright and I'm tired. The church is pretty all lit up like that. Catholic churches go all out for Christmas, always. I guess midnight mass is over and I missed it.

This was my favorite part of Christmas Eve with Mommy. My sisters and I would be all excited because we did not have to go to bed early. We would get dressed up in our Sunday best and wait patiently until it was time to go. When we would get there, it would be simply amazing.

What pretty lights. I can sit here on the steps awhile. I am sure all the parishioners have gone home.

The angels are beautiful, too. It's been so long since I called her Mommy. She hasn't been my Mommy in a long time. I guess I will sit here for a minute because I am so tired- mentally, physically, and spiritually. I am so sleepy...

"Ma'am are you ok? Ma'am? Father, I think we need an ambulance."

The Hospital

I woke up startled and looking around wildly as I was trying to determine where I was. Panicking, I tried to get up but couldn't. My attempts to move made me realize there were tubes stuck in my arms. An IV? Hospital? How did I get here? I pondered, struggling to make sense of it all. I yelled for the nurse.

"You're awake. How are you feeling? Can you tell me your name?"

"Where am I?" I asked not sure that I knew who I was and really not sure if I wanted her to know.

"Mercy Hospital."

"Mercy Hospital?" I repeated. "How did I get here?"

"By ambulance two nights ago." She responded curtly. "You had cuts and bruises all over yah. Black eye, too. But your hands were the worse. We thought you were seriously injured because of all that blood. What happened honey?"

"Two nights ago…" I repeated. "Blood? Whose blood?" Everything felt surreal. How could I be in the hospital? Unable to remember how I got here I began to question, my identity and if I even had family. Suddenly, I realized I couldn't remember a thing. I shook my head back and forth trying to clear my mind's fog but it didn't help. Samuel was the only thing I could remember. Helpless and frustrated I fell back to sleep.

Later on I awakened once more and my body ached all over. My heart reflected the room's mood, heavily draped in gray. The back wall displayed a failed attempt to help spruce up the place. The wallpaper was covered with pale pink flowers. You could tell it once was vibrant. Now the flowers just looked sad and instead of adding light, it only made the room homely. I felt lonely. The atmosphere surrounding me reeked of death.

My head was foggy and clogged. I shook my head back and forth as if by doing this I could break through the fog. I couldn't. I could only remember the name Samuel. I tried to remember who I was. Then suddenly it hit me, I didn't want to know. Intuition led me to believe that whoever I was and wherever I had come from was not a happy place. Sadness descended upon me like an ominous and I did the only thing I could do, sleep.

"*I'll kill you, you yellow bitch.*" *Visions of me running as he grabbed the back of my shirt played out in my dreams. I could see myself clearly as I hit the floor hard and received a blow to my jaw. "Crack!"*

I woke up, my gown drenched in sweat, as if I were in the fight of my life. Everything was still foggy. I didn't know if I was dreaming or awake but I hoped I was dreaming.

Not recognizing my surroundings, I suddenly realized I was in a different room. It was equally as drab and depressing as my previous room, only this time there was someone in the bed next to me. Sitting upright, I stared at her, but could not get my mind to focus. Strangely enough, I did not know who I was looking at.

"What you looking at?" She hissed at me. Saying nothing, I just stared at her. There was so much anger in her words. The harshness of her tone was unexpected. Miss Tough had caramel complexion, her petite frame was crowned with wildly matted black and brown hair. Despite the blankness in her gaze, there was warmth in her eyes. Although young, the creases permanently etched in her face indicated she had a rough life.

"I asked you what you looking at?" She hissed again.

"Why are you so angry?"

"You should be too. You stuck in this nut ward too."

"Nut ward?" I replied with a crooked grin. The drugs they gave me were so powerful that everything appeared to me in 3-D. Even the young woman's speech dragged as if she spoke in slow motion.

"Oh, I forgot them drugs they give you really mess your head up. Next time just act like you takin' 'em and then spit them out when the nurse leave. If you don't you won't be able to make sense out of nothing." She said almost motherly. Listening to her with disbelief, I could do nothing other than look at her as if she was crazy. I knew I wasn't crazy. Did she say nut ward as in psyche ward? My head hurt too much to think at that point and I was too exhausted to respond. Turning over, I fell fast asleep. It was peaceful when I slept, until the voices returned. Broken images flashed through my mind and I struggled to recall what happened to me.

When I woke up hours later, the girl in the next bed was staring at me as if she could read my mind. Strange. Just strange. I thought. "Yes?" I questioned with irritation.

"I'm just wondering why you here. I mean, I know why I'm here but you don't look the type." She answered.

"Why are you here?" I asked her. I wasn't ready to talk about myself and I didn't understand why I was even here at the moment.

"I tried to kill myself." She uttered nonchalantly. I got the impression that she was here for far more than just trying to kill herself. "And they say I tried to kill someone else in the process."

"Why did you try to kill yourself? Did you try to kill someone? You seem very smart and you are very pretty. What happened?" I asked.

"I don't feel so pretty or smart either." After a long pause, she said, "I haven't heard that I was pretty in a long, long time." The sadness in her voice almost made me cry and suddenly, I felt sorry for her. Her life must have been horrible, I thought. She never really acknowledged whether or not she tried to kill someone or not. At that point, I figured we were in the same boat. We couldn't remember or didn't want to remember, one of the two.

"So what happened?" I asked gently. I could sense that she needed someone to talk too.

"Tommy, that's my man. We been together for eight years. We ain't married though. Well, he said he was leaving me. I couldn't bear him leaving me. But he say that all the time. He say if he leave me I would be lost without him. He say I wouldn't be able to survive. I've heard that almost every day for the last eight years. So I didn't half believe him, 'cuz he say he gon' leave but never do. But this time it was different."

After a long pause I asked her "Why was it different?"

She looked at me intently as if struggling with herself to find the words to say. Finally she said simply, "His bags were packed" and looked away.

"Who's Samuel?" She suddenly asks.

"Samuel?" I say.

"Yeah, you were saying his name over and over in your sleep."

"Oh." I say, contemplating if I should explain it to her. I didn't want to let anyone know that I suddenly remembered a small portion of my dismal life. Strangely, I wanted to stay here. I wanted to rest. I didn't want to think about all the hurt and pain I had experienced. I felt a kinship with this girl. I sensed that she needed me. It is so nice to be needed.

I heard myself talking but it didn't sound like me. I began to tell her the story of the Smooth Criminal; the man who stole my heart and discarded it as if it was meaningless.

Smooth Criminal

Chocolate dream sexing my mind. You are my world my life my love of all time. I gave you my heart, my sweet valentine. You told me you loved me but hated my body and my mind. You said you loved me but couldn't stand being in the same space, place or time with me. You said you cherished me but if I looked like Susan I would be the woman of your fantasy. With that I must agree if I changed my hairstyle my eye color I would be just fine. You wanted me to change the way my thighs rubbed and my sway from side to side. You stole my soul, my heart and my pride. Chocolate dream sexing my mind.

I recited that poem to her from the depths of my soul. I don't really remember writing it and here it was spewing from me like vomit.

I took to writing poetry because I needed another outlet to express my feelings. They were mainly dark feelings because I felt depressed all the time. I wanted it all to end. I hadn't thought about suicide since my senior year in high school. Now it was on my mind all the time. Poetry gave me an outlet. Instead of killing myself I could write about it, make it poetic and no one would think I was crazy or suicidal.

I began to remember those days of total frustration when I would try to forget my sadness by reading. I would read everything I could get my hands on so as not to think about my horrible life and the circumstances surrounding it.

Reading was not helping, especially since I was feeling lots of anger and betrayal at the time. When I put my words down on paper, it felt good. It felt liberating. I could manipulate the words. I was in control of the words. Unlike my life, I could make the words do what I wanted them to do. I couldn't control my life, it was unraveling and I felt helpless.

I still remember that day. My meltdown was inevitable.

It was Juneteenth and I really didn't want to go to the celebration. I was finally getting a chance to spend time with my husband who had been missing in action lately. "We'll go out to dinner after we stop by the park. I just want to show the fellas the Expedition." He talked me into getting this gaudy vehicle that looked like a submarine. I could barely drive the thing. I thought our Jeep Cherokee was just fine.

"Ok." I said. I thought I would put on something alluring but not too sexy. I had a form fitting tank top with matching jean short shorts that accentuated my athletic legs, small waist and tight butt. I wanted my husband to desire me again.

"Are you ready yet?" he said exasperated.

"Yes, here I come." I felt I looked stunning. Samuel said nothing. He barely even looked at me. I always get nervous when he gets like that. He usually starts an argument with me, blames me for something or puts me down with menacing remarks. Like the time he told me he wished I didn't have to be four-eyed. He asked why I couldn't have perfect vision like he did. He felt that I should have no flaws.

Samuel was the type of person who had to have the best care, the freshest clothes and the best-looking woman. Instead of keeping up with the Jones' he was leading the pack. He made me feel bad about myself. After awhile, he had me thinking, yeah why couldn't I have perfect vision?

We got to the park and he immediately went to find his friends and left me standing there, yelling over his shoulder: "There's the food. I see Lee."

"But aren't we going to dinner? I said.
He walked off pretending not to hear me. He had this planned all along I said to myself. He never intended to spend time with me. He just wanted to get to the park to ditch me. He knows I would never make a scene in public. I turned away embarrassed. I sat and talked to some friends I knew for a while. Making small talk as I was trying to forget about the nice quiet dinner we were supposed to have.

I went to the food table. Yuck. The food was all picked over. I didn't eat anything. I walked back to my friends, empty like I felt. My heart and stomach filled with nothing but air.

After an hour or so, I got really pissed off. How dare he just leave me here as if I'm nobody; tossed aside like a used rag that he just cleaned his truck with. I went to go find him. He just got back from giving all of his boys a joy ride in our new Expedition.

"Samuel" I yell. "Are you ready to go? I'm hungry."

He turned to me and said, "There's food over there."

"Yes, but it is all picked over and besides, we were supposed to go to dinner."

"I changed my mind. You better go over there and get you something to eat 'cuz we ain't going nowhere else today."

I turned away. I didn't want them to see the tears forming in my eyes. As I walked away, all I heard was uproarious laughter. I turned back around, just in time to see his boy Lee give him a high five. "You sure told her!" He said laughing hysterically.

I was humiliated and furious. My feelings were crushed. Normally I don't make scenes in public because I was raised not to air my dirty laundry in public. Instead, I would wait until I got home to have an argument. That way, I save face in front of friends. I couldn't take it anymore. This mistreatment had gone on for the last nine years. I was exhausted with pretending that everything was ok.

The battle between Samuel's friend and me was constant and I usually took the back seat. Samuel had this desperate need to validate himself through the eyes of his friends. He had to look like he was the man, as if he had everything under control. He had to be the go to man with all the answers.

In his need to be the man he usually stepped on the people he felt were weak. He felt I was weak. In his eyes, I needed to be led around by the nose. I needed to be taken care of because I didn't know how to take care of myself.

I was tired of trying to prove myself to him. I worked so hard to prove to him that I was worthy of his love. I believed by just being myself, it would show him my true worth but that was not enough.

"Everybody out" I yelled. I turned to Samuel and said. "Give me the damn keys. I can go to dinner without you!"

I got into the Expedition, praying that I didn't wreck this huge monster. With tears streaming down my face, I drove around for hours trying to figure out what I did that was so wrong. I was good to him. I did everything he asked of me. It still wasn't enough. I knew this was the beginning of the end.

He came home the next morning pissed off at me because I embarrassed him in front of his boys. Dammed if I was embarrassed.

"I can't stand you. You make me sick." He said in this cold-hearted voice. At first I didn't recognize it or him.

"Whatever." I said shaking in my own skin. I have never seen him so angry. I wasn't sure what he would do.

"You fucking bitch." Angrily, he marched into the guest bedroom and slammed the door in my face.

I was in shock. He never called me a bitch before. Filled with disbelief, I went to bed broken. That night I had a fitful time tossing and turning. I finally fell into a deep dark sleep. I felt myself fall into the dream state, the place where you were half-awake and half-asleep. The devil suddenly appeared. He wanted me, my life. "Come to me", he beckoned. Terrified, his demons began taunting me. They danced around me while shooting flames of fire at me. The Devil hovered over me as if wanting to devour me. I tried to scream but I couldn't. My scream was caught in my throat. He put his hand over my mouth and nose. Clawing at his hands, my breath was leaving me fast. I felt myself starting to slip into unconsciousness. I was trying to wake up but couldn't. I struggled and fought with the devil but couldn't escape. He was telling me over and over again that I belonged to him.

Suddenly another entity appeared. He yelled, "Get out of this house!" The Devil shrieked and disappeared. The entity shined a bright light over me and said you are safe for now. But take heed, leave this place or you will lose your soul.

My eyes opened suddenly. I looked around trying to figure out where I was. Nothing looked familiar. Sweat was dripping from my entire body. I was shaken up. I didn't know what the entity meant. Was he telling me to leave my house? Was he telling me to leave my husband? Was he telling me my husband was a part of the Devil's army? I couldn't take it anymore.

Creeping into the guest bedroom with Samuel, I climbed into bed with him. There was a sense of doom hovering over me and I just didn't want to be alone.

Samuel didn't acknowledge me. I snuggled closer to him and inhaled his freshly showered scent. Just one whiff of his ocean breeze scent made me feel safe. I tried to hug him but he pushed me away. My body trembled and I wanted to cry but I knew that would only make matters worse. Samuel would get up and leave. I wanted so desperately to be held.

I lay there with this eerie feeling that my dream was a premonition. I felt the end was near but couldn't put my finger on what the end would be. Premonitions usually mean something bad is about to happen. I should have paid closer attention to the signs.

The beginning of the end

My mind went back to the first time Samuel Brent aka Smooth Criminal first thought about marrying me. He had planned the entire thing. We were to get married on Valentine's Day and he called his mother to let her know. He planned the details with his boys. But the funny thing about it, he never informed me. I was the last person in the loop to know my wedding date. That was typical of our life together. I was insignificant. I didn't matter. I should have seen the signs...

Cool, calm, collected were the words running through my head when Samuel walked through the door. I was partial to chocolate and that he was. He possessed an east coast b-ball swagger that made me stand up and take notice. Samuel was hot in a cool, funky sort of way. He had this aura that commanded respect. All hail to the king. He had a God like complex but I failed to realize it at the time.

I thought he was the messiah walking here on earth. I met him at a fraternity function when I was eighteen, fresh out of high school and my daddy's house. My daddy was very strict. We didn't date and we barely talked to boys on the phone. Daddy had to keep us locked up at home so we couldn't see his indiscretions. When you are from a small town, everyone has the opportunity to know everyone else's business. I was ripe for the picking; perfectly fresh in my naivety, a quality Samuel preyed on.

We met at a gathering for his fraternity, the pretty boys as they were called. My friends and I thought it would be a good idea to become little sisters to the fraternity. That way we could get into all the cool parties for free. They pledged the little sisters as if they were joining a real frat or sorority.

We were all down in Samuel's basement for the naming ceremony in which they give you your line name and choose who will be your mentor. Samuel gave me my name, "Irresistible". Wow, someone thought I was irresistible! I was always so awkward looking in high school. My sisters all looked so much better than me. I wore huge eyeglasses that covered fifty percent of my face. Looking back, I guess I wore them to hide me. I didn't like the way I looked. I felt that everyone thought I was hideous. From that point on I was simply infatuated with Samuel.

We started dating after the first frat party of the year signifying the start of the college party season. Being my first college party as a college freshman, I remember how excited I was. Having been sheltered all my life, I didn't know what it felt like to have such freedom. I felt grown up and empowered to make my own decisions. For the first time in my life I was free and could talk to anybody I wanted.

While dancing with Samuel's friend Carlos, he came up to us and said, "Carlos let me cut in. I am with this because all you gon' do is fuck it up." What a beginning. That should have been a sign but I was infatuated.

From that point on, we spent most of our time together. Samuel created an atmosphere of fun and games everywhere he went. He liked to joke a lot and we had a good time the first few months. Then he started disappearing. He loved to play basketball, one of the legal activities he participated in. So just to spend time with him I would go to the gym and watch him play.

One day, the games went so long that it was dark when they finished playing. He walked out of the gym without me. I went outside and saw him sitting in a car with some thug lookin' niggas. "Hey, Samuel!" I yelled. "You just goin' to leave me?" I asked.

He looked at his friends and then he turned around, looked at me, smiled and said, "Sorry the car is full." He rolled up the window, laughing his ass off as I stood there; left to inhale the exhaust from the departing car.

I couldn't believe he just left me standing there. As the car faded into the distance, I realized I had to walk home in the dark by myself. I didn't think it was funny. I was so shocked I wanted to cry. I held my tears until I got to my dorm room. As soon as I entered the room and closed the door my tears started flowing. Humiliated by someone I thought loved me, it should have been sign number two but my heart wouldn't listen. I was insecure. All my life my mother made me feel I wasn't good enough for her love. Like Cinderella, I was always trying to seek approval just to feel loved. I was honored a man of his caliber would choose me. It was a sign that he loved me. I convinced myself that this was nothing. I let that one slide.

First Breakup

After my sophomore year, Samuel and I moved in together. I attended school during the summer but couldn't afford a place of my own. I didn't want to go home. At twenty years old, my parents still treated me like a child and held me to a curfew! I was afraid to tell my parents I would be living with a boy but I was more afraid of what Samuel would think of me if I didn't. They were furious with me but what the hell. It was my life and about time I started living it.

I can't really remember the circumstances surrounding our first major break-up. I think it was because I grew tired of Samuel running the dorms searching for other women while I was left alone, paying all the bills, and having strange women call my house hanging up on me. It started to wear on me.

I was always sitting alone in our roach infested college apartment surfing illegal cable channels spliced from our neighbors upstairs. My life had become depressing as Samuel and I did nothing together anymore. I was seriously depressed. I hated sitting here alone. I sometimes thought Samuel should have majored in drama because he always put on a show.

We continually had major blow ups about his incessant need to run the dorms with his boys. All they were doing was searching for girls to sleep with.

My heart wouldn't let me believe that was what Samuel was doing. I was in denial. I wanted to believe he was good and good for me. Deep down I knew he wasn't.

My love for him suspended me in total denial about his wrongdoing.

After our fight, Samuel didn't come home that night. I found myself I clicking off the TV and going to bed alone, again. I guess he wasn't coming home again tonight.

As I climbed into bed, I heard the door lock click. My heart skipped a beat. I waited anxiously for Samuel to come in. I was hoping he returned to apologize. I wanted to kiss and make up. I didn't like all this strife between us.

I went to the door to meet Samuel, to my surprise; he walked in with a crooked smile on his face, trailed by one of his frat brothers. As insultingly as he could, Samuel spewed, "I just came to get some clothes. "Oh", was all I could say.

He continued, "By the way Jasmine I'm moving out". He slammed the key down on the glass table for emphasis and walked out of the door laughing with his frat brother.

Lying there for what seemed like hours crying a river of tears, I felt my heart being pulled apart. I half expected him to walk back through the door telling me he was sorry but I knew that wouldn't happen.

"Hold up girl," I said to myself. *"How in the hell is this motherfucker gon' tell me that he's moving out of my damn house!"* I went to the closet, grabbed a handful of his shit and before I knew it, I threw them out the front door into the hall. The precious red and white cane, symbolic of the fraternity that has been the bane of our existence hit the ground hard when I threw it outside the door. *"That bastard! I pay for this shit in here. Who the hell do he think he is?"* An hour later, everything Samuel owned was in the hall. I didn't care. I hoped somebody would come along and take all that shit!

"Hey sis."

"What's wrong?"

"Damn can't I just call my sister to see how she's doing?"

"I know you, something's wrong. What the hell has he done now?"

I got real quiet. I knew she didn't approve of our relationship.

"Well, what did the bastard do now?" She repeated.

I hated when she called him a bastard. I am the only one entitled to do that! But I had to eat crow and suck it up. I needed her to come get me before Samuel came back and wanted to whip my ass. I finally broke down and told her everything. She hopped in the car immediately to come get me. She was upset and angry. She cussed me out the entire way to her school. After the fist thirty minutes I was angry and wanted her to shut the hell up. We still had another hour to go.

No sooner then we got inside her dorm room her phone was ringing. "It's for you," She yelled.

"Who is it?" I mouthed. I didn't tell anyone that I was leaving or where I was going for that matter.

"The bastard." She replied.

"How did he get your number?"

"How should I know? Do you want to talk to him or not?"

I hesitated. I knew I shouldn't talk to him but I also wanted to hear his voice. I missed him already.

"Hello" I said reluctantly.

"Jas I am so sorry. I messed up. Come home." He said. I wasn't expecting that. I didn't know what to say so I simply said "No." I was trying to be hard even though my heart was melting

"I'm coming up there. We need to talk."

An hour and a half later he was there. I had a stone face when I opened the door for him but inside I was smiling. Driving all the way to my sister's school proved he loved me. I left with him that night, excited about the possibility for the rest of my life with Samuel.

What I thought would be a new beginning, turned in to me enduring three more years of him dissing me for his friends, and him staying out all night claiming he was hanging out with the fellas when deep down I knew it wasn't true.

I endured three more years of him telling me that I was weak and a follower. Day after day, he chiseled away at my self-esteem by telling me I was fat. I already weighed 120 lbs. He told me I needed to change my eye color to hazel. My eyes were already light brown. Samuel told me I needed to grow my hair longer because then, I would look better. To me, it meant I would look like a white girl.

I endured three more years of him getting mad at me for no reason and him torturing me by giving me the silent treatment for days. Samuel's respect for me was so far gone that he would empty his pockets full of girls' phone numbers when he strolled in between three or four o'clock in the morning.

Samuel's ill treatment of me was so intense I actually believed him when he told me I needed to be taken care of because I couldn't take care of myself. This life of mine was going nowhere fast. All I could do to survive the day was submerge myself in my schoolwork and my part-time job. I got serious about finding that perfect job after I graduated. It would be another six months before I would officially become an adult.

By this time, I had become oblivious to everything happening around me. I didn't want to know what Samuel was doing and so I withdrew into myself.

I was so shocked when I got that call. The call that changed the way I felt about Samuel. Not consciously but somewhere in the recesses of my mind, I knew Samuel wasn't the man for me. "Hello." I said.

"Is Samuel in?" the voice said.

I replied, "No he's not."

The voice said "well can you, you know get me some of that."

"What?"

"Can you sell me some stuff'?

"What in the hell are you talking about?"

"Oh, my bad. I'm sorry I will try to catch up with Samuel."

I hung up the phone. Finally everything was coming together. I couldn't figure out how he was able to buy that big screen TV and that play station. He told me his father gave him the money but I knew that was a lie. His father worked as a maintenance man with the housing authority back east. I am sure he didn't have that kind of money for frivolous things. What a joke the so-called promise ring he bought me turned out to be - to have, to hold to go to jail!

Samuel came home early that night. I was still reeling from the phone call I got earlier.

"Hey baby, I came home early so we can hang out?"

He had the stench of cheap flowery perfume and day old sweat on him as if he was drinking the night away in a five-dollar whorehouse and every inch of him reeked of alcohol.

"Come give big daddy a kiss", he said, as the rancid smell of his words attacked my nostrils.

I was totally disgusted with him for having the nerve to come in here intoxicated and smelling like some whores cheap perfume. Not to mention, I was livid to discover he was a drug dealer! Finally I said, "One of your customers called here today." He stopped dead in his tracks.

"Oh, customers?" He hesitated. I knew this was his tactic to buy him some more time to come up with a creative excuse.

"Yes. Did he track you down?"

"Jas what are you talking about? What customers?"

"Don't play stupid with me. You know damn well what I'm talking about."

"Stop playing games with me girl and tell me what you're talking about?"

"How'd you get the money for that new big screen TV?"

"My boy loaned it to me."

"Which boy? All the ones you hang with are broke."

"Damn girl, I came home early to spend some time with my baby and I get this shit!"

"What did the man want Samuel? What the fuck are you selling?"

"Don't be dumb girl. You know what the deal is. How the hell do you think you eat so good? How do you think you got this damn furniture in here or that new outfit you got last week? Didn't hear you bitching then! You can't have it both ways."

"When they come after you they'll come after me too. Did you think about that? I'm not going to jail for you." I yelled.

"Jas, it's all good. Haven't I always protected you and looked out for you? You're not in any danger. I love you too much to do that to you!" His stance softened a bit. He came closer to me opening up his arms for me to fall into and without resistance, I did. I remember thinking to myself, what a smooth criminal.

With tears streaming down my face he kissed me. He kissed away my fears. I allowed it. I did not want to lose another person I really loved. My grandmother died when I was ten and she was the only mother to me when my own birth mother could not be. I felt she was the only one that truly loved me until Samuel came along and I couldn't bear his love being torn away from me.

Graduation day arrived quickly and for me, it was an awesome day. I completed college. My family, Samuel and I were standing down in the lower part of the auditorium while I returned my gown. Everyone was looking at my degree. Being the first of my father's eight children to get a college degree, it was the first time I saw my daddy cry. We were passing my degree around and as it got to Samuel he said after looking at it "Where's the date?" He was looking for the graduation date because he was thinking if it doesn't show the date no one would know that I graduated before him. I couldn't help but to think it was so selfish of him. Even on my graduation day, the event couldn't be all about me. This should have been the third sign for me to leave but I was in love and my heart wouldn't allow me to heed them.

Hospital

Joy sat there just staring at me. I couldn't tell if she was fascinated or saddened by my revelations. She didn't say a word. I simply continued the story of the "Smooth Criminal".

Second Break Up

Our second break up was more memorable. We moved sixty miles away from our college town and I began working for a reputable company. Samuel finally graduated and was working as a corrections officer. What a crock, but then again, I guess he did understand the criminal mind.

Five years strong now and things seemed to be going well. There was no engagement ring in sight but all was good until one day, out of the blue, he lost his job. We had just moved into a plush two bedroom, two-bath apartment and it was gorgeous. It housed a spiral staircase leading to an upper office loft. Being that this was a new start and a new apartment, we simply had to have the perfect furniture - Natuzzi leather couches, a cherry wood dining room table and of course the big screen TV. We were deeply in debt.

While spring-cleaning, I found a letter Samuel wrote to his ex-girlfriend Katina. I began reading the letter and to my utter dismay, I realized it was the exact same letter he wrote to me the first year we met. I recalled how special I felt that day because I finally felt loved. Having discovered that it was never intended for me, I could do nothing more than allow devastation to consume me.

He returned that evening from having played ball all day instead of looking for a job and had the audacity to utter the words, "You didn't cook", and under his breath, "I swear you can't do shit right". I politely laid the letter he wrote me and the letter he wrote Katina in front of him and went upstairs. He followed saying, "What the hell is this? You have been going through my stuff. I can't have anything private in this damn house." Where are you going?"

My bags were packed. That morning I went out and found my own apartment. I found a cute little place across town that I could afford. I put the last of my clothes into my car and walked out, all the while my heart breaking each step I took down the stairs.

I spent the night alone and crying in my new, empty apartment. I cried for all of the heartache Samuel caused me. I cried for all of the times I gave this man a piece of my soul without demanding some of it back. I cried for my stupidity to think this man ever loved me. Despite crying myself to sleep that night, I knew that tomorrow would be a new day. This too shall pass.

I went to buy furniture the next day and I felt good. Although still sad, I was on my way to a new life. Admittedly, I did miss Samuel and felt as if I there was a hole in my heart. It was difficult after first leaving because I couldn't get him out of my system. I was torn between regaining my dignity and freedom and returning to the love of my life.

The fact that Samuel made no effort to contact me really ate me up inside. It hurt that he didn't try to get me back. Running through my mind was this tape that Samuel never loved me. I started to feel that the last five years was a total waste of my time. I was making myself crazy. After a week of this I made up an excuse to call him.

"Samuel this is Jasmine."

"Hey Jasmine. How are you?" He seemed genuinely happy to hear from me. That made me warm inside.

"I'm good. I was just calling to see if I left my black belt over there."

"No, I haven't seen it." He said.

"Oh" I said a little disappointed that he didn't say much more.

"Now tell me the truth." He continued. "You didn't call over here for a belt. You really miss me. Don't you?" He said with a laugh. All I could do was laugh with him.

"You caught me," I finally said.

"I miss you too." He said quietly.

I went over there the next day. We talked everything over. He apologized. We made love. We were back together, just like that. Being that he lost his job, I allowed him to move in with me. It wasn't long before he returned to his criminal ways. I believe he never stopped. It was such a display of naivety on my part.

The Wedding

James and Toni, the couple we did our proverbial couple thing with, were getting married. He proposed to her after having dated a little less than a year. I was crushed. We were together six years and I didn't even have an engagement ring.

No one wanted to tell me about their engagement and when I did learn of it, I couldn't believe it. We were riding in the back seat of James' car on our way to the movies.

"Toni congratulations on your engagement", I said. "I am happy for you. Let me see the ring." She raised her hand and showed me the most beautiful 2 carat round solitaire in a platinum setting, I'd ever seen.

"I was afraid to tell you about it", Toni replied.

"Why?" I asked, confused at what she meant by that.

"Well I know you and Samuel have been dating for a long time and he hasn't asked you yet." Toni's bold response slapped me in the face. I was forced to hold back any outward signs of envy. Openly, the only thing I could say was what a pretty ring. Internally, I was dying of jealousy.

That night Samuel suggested that we should start planning our wedding. I looked at him in disbelief. I knew he only said that because he saw the hurt in my eyes when I saw Toni's ring. At this point, I was at a crossroad. Should I be joyous because he finally agreed to marry me no matter what the circumstances were? Or should I tell him to go to hell? To make matters worse he never officially proposed to me!

I didn't say anything after that. I figured, finally we were getting married, so what the hell. It made me feel as if I were the happiest woman alive. We decided to be married on the date of our seventh anniversary, October 17. We started dating six years ago on that day.

We planned an intimate wedding at an adorable mansion we found in the heart of the city's country club area. The country club area was a quaint part of the city with huge oak trees and sprawling mansions covered in ivy. The mansion had a beautiful old fireplace with a marble mantel. When we saw it we both nodded our heads in agreement and knew that was the place to have our nuptials.

The mansion also had a piano room with a white baby grand in the center. I became excited imagining how I would look in my form fitting laced wedding gown that fanned out behind me, next to that piano. We decided on an elegant color scheme consisting of a very rich red, white and black. Each invitation would display a single rose to signify our enduring love and our selections for bridesmaids and groomsmen was complete.

We fought constantly during the three weeks leading up to the wedding, Samuel, "you're not putting enough money in for this wedding!" I have been spending all of my money." I whined. I was getting totally frustrated and a little scared.

"What have you paid for?" He spat at me. "Tally everything you bought cause I know you haven't spent more than me." Like a dummy I was sitting there totaling everything I spent on the wedding just to prove to him that I spent just as much money as he did. It went on like that for weeks but I did not let that deter me from experiencing the one day that every little girl dreams of. I was getting married.

The bachelor party was billed as the party of the century. Samuel had dancers, or professional strippers lined up. He had to appear big time so he rented a plush hotel ballroom. The hotel was very elegant and located in the middle of town. It should have never been used for what Samuel intended it for. This prestigious hotel was transformed into this thugged-out sleazy player's ball.

It was "Sammy's last stand". Samuel considered himself the big man on campus. Because of this he held his bachelor party in our college town despite the fact we had been out of school for a few years.

Samuel, feeling compelled to show he was big time, deliberately chose the hotel that sat in the middle of town. Between the 'video dancers', as he preferred to refer to the strippers as, and the pimp juice that was flowing, thugs and ho's lined up around the block just to check out this cities first player's ball.

It was a citywide party that everyone received an invitation to, everyone except me. Toni got it into her head that she wanted to go to the party because James would be there. They were newly married and I guess she wanted to check up on her man. I had a bad feeling about it so I didn't want to go. Toni managed to convince me to attend the party with her. Supposedly, the real bachelor set would take place after the party was over so Toni was really concerned about what was going to happen afterwards.

Samuel was all about the dollar so he began letting thug nigga's in the party. Soon afterwards, people started running. A loud bang rang out. Somebody started shooting and complete mayhem ensued. Guests were ducking and running for cover. Toni began running into the melee saying, "I got to go find my husband." I managed to snatch her and pull her into the restroom just as a flying chair whizzed by her head.

The few moments we waited there felt like an eternity. The hotel was surrounded by police when we finally walked out of the bathroom. No one could get in or out. The streets were blocked off. Toni and I stood there wondering what to do next. We couldn't leave because the police were blocking all exits.

Finally James came down from one of the hotel rooms to find us. I remember standing there dumbfounded wondering what to do. I thought he came just to get Toni. I was thinking, where is Samuel? Why didn't he come for me? James said to me "Come on Jasmine, you're coming too."

We went upstairs to their rooms. Samuel was there. Still dazed, I discreetly asked him why he didn't come looking for me. He said nastily "this was my party if I would've gone down there I could've gotten arrested and besides you weren't supposed to be here. You were not invited."

I stood looking out the window, hurt that after all that just happened; I still didn't mean anything to him. My being safe was of no concern to him. As I stood there watching all of the police activity below and seeing all the chaos, a part of my heart died and was lost to him forever. I couldn't help wonder if my life would be like this with Samuel. Would I be sitting at home with the kids in the dark because the lights were shut off for the third time that year while, the kids would be screaming they were hungry? Would I be subjected to mass chaos, anger and emptiness?

Toni and I drove home that night in silence. I was deep in thought about my life and whether or not I was making the biggest mistake of all. She was relieved James was safe and content that they could go back to living their happy little lives together.

Over the next week, the message "I should call the whole thing off" kept running through my mind. But I was paralyzed by the thought of what I would do without him. Would I be able to survive? Would I be able to breathe without him? I left him twice now and I kept running back.

In the end, I decided to go ahead with the wedding because the dress was purchased, the deposit was on the mansion and the invitations were already mailed out. This was sign number four and still, I did not take heed to it.

Finally my wedding day was here-October 15th. I was unbelievably calm. I thought I would be a nervous wreck especially since I didn't get any sleep the night before. I was lost in thought. I couldn't shake the feeling that I should move on with my life without Samuel. I was afraid that if I didn't marry him I would be missing out on something. Not only that, I felt I would be alone forever. I believed Samuel when he told me no one else would want me.

Standing there gazing at myself in the mirror, I was absolutely gorgeous in my wedding gown. I fought hard to hold the tears back. I didn't want to mess up my flawlessly made up face. This was the face that showed nothing but happiness but inside was crying.

Everyone was downstairs getting into their positions, preparing for my wedding. I was getting married and I was unhappy. I kept thinking that I should leave. I felt the need to escape down the back stairs and out the back door. I needed to be free.

"Honey are you ready?" My dad said coming up the stairs. I took a deep breath and walked into a life I knew would never be happy.

The wedding was absolutely beautiful. I wore a white form fitting wedding gown that had a long flowing train attached to it. The bridesmaids were in burgundy. Samuel wanted a red and white wedding, his fraternity colors but I convinced him that burgundy was more elegant. The mansion was tastefully decorated. We had a jazz quartet playing.

Le Divorce

I'se married now! I thought after saying I do everything was magically going to be all right. I was so empty. Nothing I did felt right. I quit my job. It wasn't working for me anymore. I was not happy. I thought Samuel would take care of me but because I wasn't a big time executive any more he wanted nothing to do with me. I worked part time at a furniture store while I tried to figure out what I wanted to do. He hated me for that. I asked him to put me on his insurance so I could have medical coverage. He said no because it would cost too much.

Samuel started staying out all night. He claimed he was working. I got my dream job back in our college town with this prominent firm. Samuel was ecstatic. He could move back to our college town and hang with the homies again. He started talking to me and spending time with me again. So naturally I thought everything was going to be ok.

Seven long years we did this dance. Loving and not loving. Hating and not hating. Speaking and not speaking. We built our first house from the ground up. I figured that would keep him home and make him want to have a family with me. He did not want to have children with me because he claimed that I would get fat and loose my perfect figure. I got tired. I went to counseling. I begged him to go. I dragged him with me.

Every Sunday I prayed a long prayer for relief. One particular Sunday I was on my knees so long I couldn't get up. The next day I got a call that I felt was an answered prayer. My boss called and offered me a promotion. This new job kept me on the road constantly.

Being on the road constantly provided some relief, but the dreams started. I had this dream that Samuel was screwing some brown-skinned girl with long hair in my house. I couldn't shake the dream. I accused him of having an affair. We had a really bad argument about my accusation. He started to sleep in our guest room.

Samuel gave me the silent treatment for three days. On that third day I could not take it anymore. I was distraught. I was crying hysterically. I locked myself in my room, planning to take my own life. I was so dazed and out of it. Rummaging through my medicine cabinet, I screamed," I don't have a damned thing in here to take my life with!" I panicked. I got a sharp knife. I couldn't find a razor. Tears were streaming down my face. I looked up and there was the bible my sister gave me the day before. I picked it up. I read Psalms 91. I prayed, "Lord protect me. Show me your will. Be my comforter and my strength when I am weak. Protect me from the enemy." I went to sleep that night knowing that everything will eventually be ok because I had God with me, protecting me.

We had our last counseling session. The counselor was asking about our finances and how we shared paying the bills. Samuel made way more money than I did. She wanted to know why we were splitting everything fifty-fifty. I tried to explain that he never has any money. She asked him where all the money was going. He said that he put the bulk into his retirement account. She asked why if you are struggling to pay bills. I listened intently as I wanted to know the answer to that question as well. He yelled out "Because I don't want her to get her hands on any of my money." I fell silent. The counselor fell silent. We left the session not talking not even looking at each other.

My counselor called me the next day to see if I was all right and if I needed something to help me sleep since I was having sleepless nights. She asked a very poignant question, was I ready to make a decision about my marriage. Was my marriage worth saving? She left that message on the answering machine.

I thought all night about what Samuel said about his money. I thought about how I gave every penny that I earned to keep us afloat and keep us happy. I thought about how much I put into this relationship to keep it going. I was offered a transfer to Atlanta with my job. I wasn't sure if I was going to take it. I wanted my relationship to work. Then I started to think that maybe if both of move we would have a fresh start. With just the two of us there and not knowing anyone we would be forced to deal with each other and possibly build a stronger relationship.

I called my counselor to let her know that I wouldn't need any drugs to help me sleep. I called my boss and told him I would take the transfer. Samuel was furious. He did not want to leave. He wouldn't talk to me for a week. I finally told him I was leaving with him or without him. I left the next day for a business trip. I would be gone for three weeks. In between that time I went to Atlanta and found an apartment to live in.

Some years later I found out the reason he did not want leave and move to Atlanta. He had a girlfriend of seven years, April. She had long flowing hair; hazel eyes and was very thin. She was biracial. This is how Samuel wanted me to look like.

April was in the picture from the time we got married. I also found out that she was even at our wedding. It was because of her he treated me cruelly. It was because she had long hair and was thin as a rail that I had to be also. It was because he couldn't see her when he wanted to he would give me the cold shoulder and not talk to me for weeks on end.

Atlanta was great there were black people everywhere. Living in Nebraska was like living in

Whiteville. This was refreshing change of pace. Although Samuel was not fully on board with the move he was supposed to wait until the house sold and then he would move. When the house sold he did not move. He got an efficiency apartment. Now he was waiting to see if he could get a job first.

A year had passed and he still hadn't moved. Then he was arrested. All the years of his criminal activities caught up with him. After six months of being out of work, depleting his bank account and retirement fund, a good attorney and a technicality he was free. He was broke.

One day out of the blue there Samuel was. He was just sitting on my doorstep to the house I had just bought in a quaint suburb in Atlanta. I said "hello" "I didn't know you were moving down."

He replied "Baby I just thought it was time for me to make that move." This was especially disheartening, after the Christmas we spent together that year. He invited his sister and son down to spend the holidays with us. I guess he didn't want to be alone with me and he figured he would really be in the doghouse if he didn't come.

That Christmas was unforgettable. He called me daily with instructions on how he wanted me to prepare for the holidays.

"Jasmine, make sure you get my son a few gifts for Christmas. Also, make sure you get something for my sister. She doesn't have anyone to get her anything."

"Ok." I said. Christmas was my favorite time of year. I was in a festive spirit therefore, I agreed to all of Samuel's demands.

I braved the horrendous Atlanta traffic to buy gifts for everyone. I didn't want anyone to be left out on Christmas morning. I planned a huge elaborate meal. Everything was set. Christmas morning came. Samuel's son was passing out the gifts. Everyone had a gift but me. I cried inwardly. I didn't want to spoil everyone's Christmas. I excused myself to go attend to the food. Two days later he was back in Nebraska.

So that day Samuel showed up on my doorstep all I could do was pour myself a stiff drink. I went upstairs and took a long bubble bath contemplating what I was going to do next. I was furious that now he wanted to come and be my husband now that his trial was over. He was also broke and jobless. After a long fight with myself, I let him stay; after all he was my husband. I figured that we could start over. That was what I wanted in the first place.

After a week, he found the basketball court. He started hanging out there instead of job hunting. One day I came home after working a twelve-hour day, my house was dirty, he cooked himself some food left none for me and he was gone out the door to play basketball. I could not believe it. This broke ass nigga in my house, eating my food, dirtying up the place, had the nerve not to fix me anything and didn't even take out the trash! Right then and there it finally clicked. He didn't care about me at all. I was just a means to an end for him!

The next day I was determined to find a divorce attorney. I didn't know anything about attorneys let alone in Atlanta. I remember sitting there praying at work "Lord I need your help. This has gone on far too long. Please help me find a good attorney." I opened the phonebook to the attorney section. I found an ad for a black female attorney. What caught my eye was the fact that she and a scripture in her add. I looked up and said "thank you lord".

I called her. She could see me that day. We went through the consultation. She told me the cost. I wrote her a check that day. She asked me if I wanted to think about it. I said no. Got back to work within the hour. I felt a weight lifted. I didn't tell Samuel that day. I wanted to wait for the divorce papers to come. I didn't want to spend the extra money to have him served. I said I would do it myself.

The papers came. It was harder than I thought. He asked me to pay three thousand dollars so he could hire a headhunter. I gave him the divorce papers and told him he had to move out. He said he wasn't going to sign the papers. I told him that I will fight him until the day he died or until he gave me a divorce. He signed the papers and left two days later. I was free. I finally took heeded all of the signs.

Through out it all I came to believe Samuel hated me. It was apparent in the end; he didn't know how to love me because he didn't love himself. He didn't respect his body; therefore, he degraded on mine. He didn't appreciate his own intelligence so he belittled mine. He didn't embrace his own uniqueness therefore he envied mine.

The lesson from Samuel was hard felt. I learned that you should always respect and be true to yourself. You can't get so caught up into one person that you lose yourself. You have to get to know yourself and develop who you are. Self-love and self-respect are essential to your very survival.

The Hospital

She just stared at me. Her face mirrored mine. Crystal tears of pain sliding down once vibrant cheeks. One at a time the tears baptized our folded hands in perfect syncopation. She knows too well this pain. How could she? She's so young. She could be no older then twenty-five. I don't like this one bit. I don't like this mask of pain I see in her eyes, eyes like mine showing only utter disappointment, discouragement and despair. I could understand mine. I'm twelve years older then she is. I have been around a little bit to know this pain. She hasn't.

I never really told that story before. It felt freeing to tell it. Lord knows I had several more to tell. "Well" I said to the girl in the next bed, "Since you know some intimate details about me at least you can tell me your name."

"I'm Joy." She said her sadness lurking. I got the distinct feeling she has never known joy.

"Joy" I repeated. It was as if I knew her or we were somehow connected or should be connected. It was weird. She was vaguely familiar.

"I'm Jasmine, but don't tell anybody I know who I am. I'm not ready to leave yet."

"Why, you want to stay in this nut house?" She said.

"I am so, so tired. I just want to rest. I don't know what happened to me before I got here. I just need some time to figure out what happened. Somehow I feel I would be better off dead."

"Sometimes I feel the same way." She said softly. "Tommy made me feel like that. I thought he was my best friend." Her voice trailed off. She was in a far off place.

Her eyes glassed over. After a long pause she said, "Tommy was a predator I was a child."

She closed her eyes tight to shut out the memories. I let her be. She suddenly started talking as if her life depended on it. At first it was a hurried whisper, then, as she continued her story her voice got stronger and more powerful. I watched Joy buoy into her own world. She floated in and out of reality. Thoughts of her shattered past danced back into her head as if they were happy little jigs that she should want to remember. She did not.

"I was born in Tuscaloosa, AL. I was the second child out of eight. My mommy was a hoe. Simple as that! All but two of us had the same daddy. My older sister was just like my mommy and ran away with the first no good nigga that flashed a little bit of cash at her. Now I hear that bitch is trickin' on the street like some common two bit whore, trickin' for her next fix. What a waste. She was so smart".

I just stared at Joy. She needed to get this out. So much anger, so much pain I sensed from her. Joy continued.

So since my mommy was out ho'in and my older sister was out ho'in, taking care of the household and all those bad ass kids fell on me. Lawd knows I tried my best with them but they were wild.

Her voice trailed off and I could tell she was back stuck in her past.

Joy

"Mommy", Joy hollered, "these are your kids you take them today. I got to go to school". School was my only haven. There, I got to be a kid. At 15, I was the mommy and daddy to my younger sisters and brothers - four boys and two girls. My older sister left a few months ago. Sissy, well her real name is Destiny but we called her sissy. All the boys called us Sissy. She just up and walked out with some sugar daddy. She was 16. He was 45.

"I got to got to go down to the welfare office. They done messed up my check again. You get these little bastards ready for school. I'm out." Mommy said, slamming the raggedy door that was already hanging by a thread on its hinges behind her. One more good slam would knock the splinted door off its hinges.

Bastards are right! None of these kids has the same daddy except JoJo and Dada who are twins. I don't know why she feels the need to go down there, Joy thought. It ain't gon' change nothing.

Joy rushed to get the kids ready and out the door she went to catch the school bus. She was determined to make it to school today. I want to see Tommy, she thought. He's one of the best English teachers I had. He didn't allow us to call him Mr. Morgan. Just Tommy he told us. He was so awesome. He really took interest in me. He enjoyed my writings. I want to show him my latest poem. I have come to depend on his opinions of my work. He makes me feel like I'm worth a damn.

"Joy I would like to see you before you leave" Tommy said as the bell rang and restless teenagers ran towards the door. I was excited. I get to spend a little time with Tommy alone. Sitting so close to him made me feel safe. I felt that nothing bad would happen to me. He was reassuring, caring and kind. I felt special around him.

"You look nice today". Tommy said.

"Thank you." I blushed. I know he was just trying to make me feel good. I had my sister's faded hand-me-down jeans on and a faded red tee shirt that didn't fit too good. I was a little busty for fifteen so I felt a little embarrassed that my shirt was so tight. He kept staring at me in my face at my shirt. I felt more embarrassed. I was mad at Mommy for not being able to buy me adequate clothing.

"You are a bright student and I think you have a special gift in your writing."

"Really!" No one has ever given me a complement before. That made me feel good.

"Yes you do." He reiterated as he placed his hand on my thigh, rubbing oh so gently. I stiffened a bit. After a while it felt good to have someone touch me affectionately. Mommy never hugged us anymore. All she did was yell and hit. We all just tried our best to stay out of her way.

"What you got here?" He leaned across me to pick up my notebook. He smelled good. He was clean cut respectable looking. Not like those bums Mommy brought home. He talked really proper like too. I liked that. I wanted to soak up every word he said. I was a sponge sopping up everything he had to offer. I hoped to be sophisticated like him one day. That's why I tried so hard in school. I didn't want to end up like Mommy or my sister.

Damn these kids are working my nerves. Where's Mommy.

"Sissy, I'm hungry"

"Where's Mommy?" I said.

"I don't know.'

"Ok give me a minute. I got to finish this assignment."

"I'm hungry" Jr. Screamed at the top of his lungs and the rest of the little ones chimed in. I had no choice but to fix dinner now. I wish Mommy would be a mother to her own damn kids!

Joy stopped talking all of a sudden like a certain memory was too hard for her to articulate. I didn't mind. My head hurt. I couldn't think any more. I couldn't take any more pain. I rolled over to go back to sleep but talking about Samuel brought back a flood of memories of the men in my life.

I realized that at thirty-seven, I have never had a good relationship. Every single one of them was bad. How could that be? I have to have a good one or at least one that was pleasurable.

I was racking my brain to think of one because if there weren't then that would make me a total looser. These drugs were making it hard to think. I stopped trying. I fell asleep just as the thought of Que Dawg danced into my head...

Que Dawg

Edward Anthony was the kind of man you fucked but never fell in love with. He stood 5'9" and had the body of Adonis! He was of the chocolate persuasion, deep, creamy and oh so irresistible. The jokester of his crew, no one ever took him seriously.

I've known him since junior high school and I could tell nothing had changed since we were kids; he was still the man all the girls wanted. We were no longer kids and what I wanted to do to him was never taught in any of the classes we attended in school.

After being married to Samuel for a year I was empty inside and all I wanted was to feel loved again, even if it was just sex.

My sister dragged me out for my twenty-fifth birthday. The thought of celebrating never occurred to me because I was feeling a little blue. My life was not the fairytale I thought it should be. Samuel was working as usual so my sister and I went to a club that was nothing more than a hole in the wall. The atmosphere was dreary and the dance floor was no larger than a child's play pin. The men in there were old cat daddies still trying to show their player's cards. They didn't have enough sense to know that their player's cards expired decades ago.

We walked in the door of the club and there he was Edward Anthony. He was this perfectly chiseled, dark specimen of a man whose body could take you on a fantastic voyage. I hadn't seen him for a while so it was great getting to know him again. We danced, talked, and flirted all night. Body heat was rising and I began losing myself in the lies he told me. All I could think about was how I wanted him to take a hold of me and ravish my body.

"Hey Jasmine, so what's up?" Edward said. "We are totally vibing, are you leaving with me or what?"

"I am a married woman." I said this while thinking how much I wanted him to take me home and rock my world.

"Yes, but are you happy?" His words hung on his sheepish grin.

"Of Course" I replied. I wondered if my answer was convincing. Did it show just after a year of marriage I was totally miserable?

"Look, I'm feelin' something, and you are too. I can see it. Here's my number. Use it any time." He said.

He folded a piece of paper in my hand and kissed me goodnight. I watched as he walked away. The sight of his tight butt and hard thighs made me want to run after him, beg him to do things to my body that hadn't been done to it in so, long.

I called after him "I'm never going to use this number!"

He laughs and said "Sure, that's what they all say; I'll be waiting for your call."

As I lay in my bed that night all I could think of was Edward. I wondered what he was doing with himself since high school. He was a star football player. He definitely didn't lose that football player's physique.

Laying next to my husband's cold snoring body, I masturbated to the thought of Edward inside of me working some kind of voodoo magic to make my emptiness go away. With every rise and fall of Samuel's chest, in deep slumber, I closed my eyes tighter and imagined the feel of Edward's tongue all over my body. By the next morning I was intoxicated with the desire of him. I had to call.

I called him that evening while Samuel was at work or whatever it was he did when he was gone. The phone seemed like it rang for an eternity but in actuality it only rang three times.

"Hello is Edward there?" I was anxious.

"This is he." This smooth voice said on the other end.

"Do you know who this is?" I said trying to sound sexy.

"Yes, I told you, you'd call." He said. I didn't want to concede just yet.

"If you know who this is say my name?" I challenged.

"Come over here and I will say your name all night. Or better yet I will make you scream mine."

That was all the encouragement I needed. I dressed in a sexy purple teddy, my high-heeled black stilettos and an easy to remove tight fitting little black dress and out the door I went.

I was nervous, excited and guilty all at the same time. I was going back and forth should I keep driving or should I turn around and go back home. I kept justifying it by telling myself that Samuel was doing the same thing, that, he didn't care about me.

I found out today that he didn't put me on his health insurance as I asked him to. I went to my doctor's office and they told me I had no coverage. I was so embarrassed.

Confronting Samuel was futile. He just looked at me with his evil grin and said, "It cost too much for me and you to be on there. So I decided it wasn't worth it."

Out the door he bounced with a sinister little chuckle. Leaving me there feeling humiliated. He made me feel as though I was of no importance to him. My heath was not his concern. He had better things to attend too.

I was working on contract now until I decided what I wanted to do. I couldn't afford my doctor's bill. In light of the fact that Samuel wouldn't put me on his insurance, it was just another bill I had to worry about.

I couldn't believe he refused to put me on there because it would cost him too much. I was forcing myself not to cry, but a lone tear slipped past my left eyelash, slowly sliding down my freshly made up cheek. Before I knew it I was sitting before his apartment complex.

The apartment complex was in the older part of town. The building was drab. It was made of a dirty brown brick. Driving up at dusk made it look more dreary and sinister. The buildings were arranged in this ominous semicircle, as if ready to attack. It was so uninviting. Was it a sign that I shouldn't even be here? Panic set in. I sat there for a while. I put the key back in the ignition. I was about to leave.

Edward opened the door. He had no shirt on and silk pajama bottoms. His chiseled chest was glistening. That twinkle was in his eye. He had an impish grin on his face that put my mind at ease.

I got out of the car and walked seductively towards him in my four inch stilettos. Edward let me in. He smelled delicious. He didn't mess around with formalities. No chitchat needed. We went straight to the bedroom. He peeled my clothes off of me. Edward said, "Turn around. Bend over". I obediently followed his command. He entered me slowly, going deeper with each stroke. It felt so good, even better than I could have ever imagined. The orgasms were too numerous to keep track of. For the first time in my life I was completely satisfied.

Afterward he held me tenderly. I didn't expect that from him. I just thought it would be done and over with. He spoke softly.

"I had so many dreams," he whispered. "I wanted to become a mega promoter. I'm a nobody. I never thought I would end up back here in this dump. I was going places. I was supposed to make things happen.

Now look at me." He stopped suddenly choking back tears.

I didn't know what to say to that. I could tell he had held that in for so long and that he needed somebody to talk to, somebody that wouldn't judge him. He needed somebody to build him up. It was apparent for the last ten years or so any and everybody that came across his path had beaten him down. I so could understand how he felt. Finally I said, "I know how you feel. It's like you had a plan of how you wanted your life to be and then suddenly you're lost and can't find your way back."

"Yeah, I should have been further along than this. My family treats me like the biggest loser. It's so hard when both your little brothers are more successful then you are. I was never the big brother to them that I should have been. I should have been the one showing them the way to success." He said with melancholy in his heart.

"Yeah, I hear you. Although I am not the oldest, being one of the oldest, I feel as though I have the weight of the world on my shoulders. I have to be the perfect example to my younger brothers and sisters. It's hard trying to be perfect, trying to pretend that everything is alright. Just so at the family get-togethers you are not put in the hot seat scrutinized for your failures" I sympathized.

"Yeah, I know." He said.

"I guess if we keep on trying and doing the right thing then we'll be ok. Besides they always say you fail forward to success so I guess you can't be successful without failures." I said trying to cheer Edward up.

"That's good advice. I'll have to remember that. You're good for something I see." Edward said playfully.

It was weird. I felt very comfortable lying in his arms. He opened up to me, something Samuel never did. He seemed comfortable with me as well. He didn't want me to leave. An incredible sadness darkened his eyes as he walked me to the door. He kissed me gently and said goodbye. My heart sank a little, partly because I was leaving Edward and partly because I had to return to my dismal life with Samuel.

The good feeling of Edward's aura didn't last for long. The next day I felt even emptier than before giving myself to Edward. The sex was awesome. Samuel has never made love to me like that. I was in a funk all day. Why couldn't my husband be that passionate with me?

Why doesn't he want to spend time with me or take interest in me the way any man on the street would? Why couldn't he just love me?

I have to admit though; being with Edward was a natural high. That was the fix I needed. I was like a junkie eagerly looking for my next fix. He taught me amazing things about sex. I did things that I never done before or felt comfortable doing. He made me feel as though my body was made to be enjoyed and admired. Samuel always made me feel like a tramp. Samuel made me feel as though my body was just there for him to gawk at and rape any time he wanted. I was his personal whore.

Edward and I would meet almost daily to get lost in each other's arms, forgetting reality if only for moment. He was running from his feelings of inadequacies in his career. I was running from the inadequacies in my marriage. It was a great arrangement. There were no strings attached. I was undoubtedly hooked.

It was raining. It was coming down so hard that it was completely dark even though it was 3 o'clock in the afternoon. The rain matched my mood perfectly. My feelings were pounding down hard on my heart. I knew I had to end it. I knew that doing dirt never stayed hidden. It was only a matter of time before Samuel found out. I had to give up my chocolate lover. Something I realized sadly I did not want to do. Edward gave me a sense of purpose for some strange reason. He accepted me as I was. He didn't demand of me anything I could not give him which made me feel special and somehow important. In return, I gave him encouragement. I told him constantly and consistently that he was a great man; that he would make it big someday as long as he believed.

As the rain came down harder, I didn't think I was going to make it to Edward's house. When I got there he had smooth jazz playing and my favorite red wine, Shiraz by Yellow Tail waiting for me. He approached me with a towel to dry me off, kissing me passionately as he was drying my hair. He was pulling me deeper into his soul. I so wanted to go there but I came over with a purpose. I had to tell this sensuous man that I was leaving town. I was moving not far but my heart could not take the guilt any more. He started kissing me more passionately as if he knew my intended purpose and he was hell bent on changing my mind.

"Wait" I said softly. "I have something to tell you."

"What is it love?"

"I am moving."

"Where?"

"Out of the city."

"How far?"

"Not far, only an hour away."

"That's nothing. We can still see each other."

"Well, we need to talk about that."

"Are you saying you don't want to see me anymore?"

He looked wounded, like I kicked him in the stomach causing him to lose his breath, gasping for air. That made me sad. I never wanted to hurt this man, who gave me so much, who seemed to love me unconditionally.

I said, "I feel so guilty. This is hard for me. I just don't know what I want."

He said, "Do you care about me?"

"Yes you know that I do."

"Then why end it? You said yourself that your husband doesn't care about you. And under his breath he said, "I know that for a fact, he's been hitting April forever."

"What repeat that?"

"Nothing, it is just that I have come to care about you. I want you in my life."

I started to cry. He hugged me. He led me to the bedroom. He slowly removed my clothes. He made the sweetest love to me. It was gentle, not like before. He made love to me like he was in love. Although it was never said he understood my pain. We both knew this was the last time we would ever make love and hold each other in each other's arms. We knew this was the end.

I have never forgotten my love affair with Edward. He taught me that my body was a temple worthy to be worshiped. He taught me that being sensual and sexy was a positive trait to have not a negative one. He said my sexuality was what he loved about me. He taught me that sensuality was a gift and that I shouldn't be ashamed of it. He also started me on my journey into me. For the first time in my life, I looked at myself as being important.

I didn't feel as if Samuel gave me my identity any more. I was finally starting to feel like a real person.

The Hospital

Joy woke up suddenly. She must have been dreaming. She looked scared, then sad. My heart went out to her. "Jasmine, have you ever been in love so bad that it hurts like hell to know that you will never be able to be with that man ever again?" She asked me.

"Yes." I said. There was nothing else I could say, just yes. Especially since I was trying to shake the bad dream I had about a river of blood that I was swimming in upstream. It makes me shudder. She looked at me blankly. For some unknown reason I felt compelled to tell her the story of Rasta as an explanation of that kind of pain she was speaking of. However my story would have to wait. She had something burning on her mind and she had to get it out. I sat there quietly waiting for her to start. Her voice was barely above a whisper. I had to strain to hear her.

Joy

He promised me that I would have a wonderful life with him. All he said was that I needed to trust him.

He said if I just trusted him he would make everything all right.

"Mr. Tommy, I have something to tell you". I said.

"Joy, you know that you can just call me Tommy. No need to put Mr. in front of it. What's on your mind?"

"Well," I hesitated because Mommy says never air your dirty laundry in public. She says to keep it in the house. But I was tired. I was tired of taking care of my brothers and sisters while her and Sissy was out chasing men. So I went ahead and told it.

"Go ahead". He encouraged. "I can see what ever this is it is wearing heavily on you and you need to bare your soul".

"Well, my mommy stays gone for weeks on end leaving me with the kids. My older sister ran away months ago. We are running out of food and money. I just don't know what to do." I said sobbing like a baby. All I could see was the sad, tired, hungry looks of my little brothers' and sisters' faces. They wanted me to make it better. I just didn't know how to do that. As Tommy put his arms around me, I cried harder. I have never been hugged before. I was sort of embarrassed by my tears. I prided myself on being hard and being strong enough to be able to handle any situation. At fifteen, I thought I was super woman.

He ushered me out of the school so quickly I didn't know what was happening. I just kept crying. I couldn't stop. He gently placed me into his black sleek Volkswagen Jetta. I had never been in a new car. I could remember thinking in between sobs. He drove slowly as if he was contemplating what to do with me. I tried, but I couldn't stop crying. The tears just gushed out of me. I held them in so long that now that they are released they didn't want to stop. It was like if I stopped crying then my tears knew they would be placed in hibernation never to show themselves again.

Tommy stopped suddenly. We were in front of a beautiful brick house. It wasn't big but it had a well-manicured yard. It had a privacy fence around it. It had evergreen bushes on both sides of the door. And the door, it wasn't sagging off the hinges. It was a real home. That made me smile a little on the inside. I finally got to see what a real home was like.

The sobs stopped but the tears kept coming. Tommy led me gently inside. It was beautiful. The fist room I saw looked like a library or something. It had so many books. One whole wall was covered with books from the floor to the ceiling. I was amazed that one person could have so many. He later told me that this room was only his office.

He took me to a bedroom. It was beautiful. It had a queen sized mahogany sleigh bed with a super high headboard. The bed actually had a paisley deep burgundy and blue comforter set on it with matching pillows. The dresser was a perfect match to the bed. It had an ornamented mirror attached that exuded elegance. I had never seen bedroom furniture like this. We had hand me down mixed matched stuff. Some days you were lucky to sleep in a bed.

He gently led me to the bed like I was a delicate flower. I thought he was just going to leave me there but he didn't. He held me close to his chest. "Just rest sweetheart we will figure out what to do later." He said. I could smell a hint of his fading Hugo boss cologne. I drifted into the most peaceful sleep. I couldn't remember the last time I slept so soundly. I felt safe in his arms. I knew nothing would harm me now. I could truly let my guard down.

Hospital

With that Joy was spent. She didn't have anything left to continue her story. I could see she was struggling with the rest of what happened to her with this man. I just let her be. I knew how it felt to feel totally safe with someone; to let your guard down and they end up hurting you beyond your wildest comprehension. Her Tommy was my Rasta.

I laid there for hours trying to figure out what went wrong with me and Rasta. I loved that man from the top of his head down to the rusted crusty curled up toenails of his callous caked feet. He was the one that I thought I would spend forever with.

"What's wrong?" Joy suddenly asked me.

I thought she was sleep. I must have been crying again. I guess both our minds were reeling from thoughts of our past.

Rasta- The Glorious Beginning

Here I am stuck outside of Fayetteville, AK with my entire life packed in a U-Haul fleeing for my life. As I sit there, lonely and alone on the side of the road waiting for the mechanic, I ponder my life thus far. I'm thirty-five years old and still can't get love right. A single tear trickles down my check. Love keeps slapping me in the face taunting me to do something about it. It laughs at me. It calls me stupid for falling for it again. It pulls at me, sucks me in and then bails on me like disappearing acts.

I can't believe he would let me drive this U-Haul truck pulling my jeep all by myself across the country. He really didn't love me. Used and abused again.

Tears flowed freely while I waited alone on the side of the road waiting in vain. Thinking back on it all, I now realize this relationship was nothing but damn good sex.

I cried uncontrollably. I was going into hysterics. What did I do to deserve this, the lying the cheating the abuse? I was good to him. I loved him with everything I had. I gave of myself completely. I didn't see the repairman come up to the window. I heard this tap. I jumped. He scared me.

"Miss are you ok?"

"Yes". I said weakly. "Are you here to fix the U-Haul?"

"Yes, I'll get started."

I dried my eyes and watched him in a daze. The sun was slowly setting. I knew that I couldn't continue my journey that day. I was so hoping that I could get home to Nebraska and be with family who actually loved me. For some reason God had me out here on this open highway, stranded and alone. Did he want me to reflect on what happened with Percy? I always thought we would get married and have babies, have a house with a white picket fence and be deliriously happy. That's what I get for believing in fairy tales. Fairy tales never come true.

I started my long journey home again bright and early the next day. I was determined to get home with a positive attitude. I was putting all the things Percy did to me behind. I was starting over. "What is that noise?" I turned the radio down. The truck started slowing down again. It wouldn't go above 35 mph. I'm familiar with this truck stop here in Joplin. I will get out and call U-haul again. Stranded again.

Perched in this drab desolate hotel room I could only do one thing; cry out to the Lord. Lord, what is it? Isn't it bad enough I'm fleeing for my life here? Can't I just get home safely? That night, alone in my hotel room, I cried. I cried for being so stupid. I cried because I missed Percy. I cried because I didn't want to go home broke and broken hearted. I cried because I should have officially broken up with him.

Then torrential anger enveloped me; took over my entire being. I screamed in utter aguish. I grabbed my wallet, took out the picture of Percy and me, and ripped it into pieces. I called him. He didn't answer. I hung up. I wrote an angry letter. I ripped it up. I lay there spent and drained. I was tired of it all. I was tired of the pain. I was tired of the sadness. I prayed for a change in Nebraska. I prayed for a 360-degree change, a total transformation, a new beginning…

It all started when I realized my marriage was beyond repair. After my divorce I lost my damn mind. It was a period of much sex and alcohol. And then I met him. I fell hopelessly in love with this no good, fake, lying cheating pseudo-want to be Rastafarian.

Percy Lovejoy aka Rasta had this old world socialist charm. His light brown eyes and dark skin were captivating. He wasn't overly gorgeous it was just something about him that made me say hmmm. His intelligence was like a cool breeze on a hot summer day. He was laid back with an easygoing attitude. I got lost in him immediately. He was my one true love. The man I would lay my life down for. He was the man I would have done anything for to keep him happy and in my life forever. He was the one I was going to spend the rest of my life with.

We met while I was on a business trip in Kansas. We worked with the same company. We knew of each other but never really interacted. Everyone was down in the lobby trying to find out what we wanted to do after we came back from dinner. We decided to get a game of spades going. I was bragging that I could not be beat! He was bragging that he was the spades king! We got a game going out by the pool. I beat him and his partner royally with a white boy from southern Alabama!

Percy and I sat out by the pool after the game sipping on drinks, I was bragging about my win and Percy eating crow. We sat there gazing into each other's eyes, talking and laughing. I talked about my impeding divorce. He told me about his wife and the fact that it wasn't going well at all. He told me that he felt that his wife was cheating on him every time he left on a business trip.

We talked about music. He told me he liked reggae. He told me that he wanted to retire in Jamaica and have a little stand on the beach. It was refreshing. Conversations with Samuel were never this easy going. It just flowed. He had the most incredible hypnotic brown eyes. I was hooked. That frightened me. I kept my distance for the rest of the conference.

Three months later we ended up in Nowhere, Oklahoma working on a project. He was the lead on this project so technically he was my boss. We were reacquainted at the infamous dinner party.

I have a problem with other people cooking my food. I volunteered to cook. I made my slammin' catfish fillets, hush puppies, fries coleslaw and we had a whole lot of alcohol to wash it down. All our co-workers were there. It was just so nice to have some real food. We had been working on this project for three weeks, eating out everyday.

We were in Percy's suite because he had the stove and refrigerator. It was also the biggest. I guess if you were the HNIC you got it like that.

People were leaving. I was pooped. Everyone was outside on the patio. I plopped my tired ass on the couch, put my feet up on the coffee table, leaned my head back on the back of the couch and closed my eyes. As the last person left Percy came over to me to see if I was all right. "Hey are you ok?"

"Yes just tired. Just give me a second and I will leave."

"Take your time. You worked hard today. The food was good by the way. You got some skills!"

"Thanks." I said.

"So why did you hang back. You know you wanted to get to know me better didn't you?" He said in his best smooth jazz voice.

Arrogant little fucker, I thought. "No just tired boo."

"You're married right?"

"Yes I am. You are too if I remember correctly."

"You are correct. So are you happily married?"

"Why do guys ask that? Does it matter, married is married."

"You have a point there."

"So are you happily married?"

"Not fair for you to ask me if you are not going to answer it."

"Touché."

"Have you ever cheated on your husband?"

I just smiled as visions of Edward Anthony danced in my head.

"Judging by that smile, I can tell that you have?" he said disturbing my thoughts.

Admitting to nothing, I asked "What about you?"

"I decline to answer that question on the grounds that it might incriminate me."

I laughed heartily. "I understand." I say. "Well let me get out of here so you can get some sleep."

He walks me to my car. "Thanks again for cooking. Oh by the way you owe me a rematch in cards!"

"That's right. Set it up and I will whip your ass again."

He smiles, gives me a hug and said good-bye. I smiled all the way to my hotel. What a nice guy I say to myself. I wonder why he's having problems with his wife.

We met for lunch the next day. He was very charming and sincere. That was rare in a man. I couldn't stop looking into those incredible hazel brown eyes. It was hypnotic. On top of that he was the perfect gentleman. He ordered for me because I had never been to that restaurant before. He was just so sweet and attentive. I guess I was just used to Samuel leaving me behind not caring about my wants or needs.

My heart was melting. I longed for a man to take interest in me and show a little tenderness towards me. Hell I will just take a man showing me a little kindness at this point. Percy was showing me that. I liked it and I liked him.

The next day we all planned to go to dinner to celebrate the completion of the project. That evening when I went back to my hotel room to change for dinner, my phone was ringing. "Hello" I said as I snatched the phone from its cradle.

"Jasmine this is Samuel, your husband or did you forget you have one?"

"How could I ever forget that?"

"You put our house up for sale?"

"Yes, You are not going to have your hoe in my house?"

"What the hell are you talking about? I don't have anyone else."

"Well there must be a reason you don't want to move to Atlanta with me. I can't imagine that it's because of your boys. What is she pregnant? Is that why you never wanted to have a baby with me?"

"You're losing it."

"Why do you always call me crazy when I ask you these questions?"

"Because you are crazy. Where do you get this stuff? How could you put our house up for sale without telling me?"

"The same way you sent all of your mail to Robert's house to hide how much money you make."

"Who told you that?"

"I see that you're not denying it you just want to know who told me."

"Well you obviously believe it so it doesn't do me any good to deny it."

"You know this conversation is becoming trite, I am hanging up."

"What about the house?"

"What about it? I can't afford to pay a house note in Lincoln and pay for my apartment in Atlanta."

"What about me?'

"What about you, you decided you didn't want to be with me the day you let me move to Atlanta alone." Click I hung up. I was tired of the conversation.

Ring. I snatched the phone. "What Samuel, What?"

"Sounds like someone is angry." This sultry voice said on the other end.

"Just a little. Who's this?"

"Forgot my voice already?"

"Oh Percy, Sorry just having a heated conversation with my not so significant other."

"Oh I'm sorry to hear that. Is everything ok? Can I do anything for you?"

"No I am fine. I am really not in the mood to go to dinner with everyone."

"Do you want me to bring you something?"
"No that's ok. I'll be fine but thank you for caring."

That night Percy brought me a prime rib dinner with the works any way. It also included dessert.

"Thank you for the food. How much do I owe you?"

"Don't worry about it. It's on me. Well I can see that you are not it best spirits so I am going to leave you to your dinner. Call me if you want to talk."

Percy hugged me and left. It would be so nice to have a man like that. I don't know why his wife doesn't see it.

The following week, Percy wined and dined me as if he was trying to make up for what Samuel did not do. We found a little hole in the wall jazz spot to chill at. He said he was only listening to jazz because of me. He claims to be a diehard blues fan; but I could tell he was digging it.

Somewhere between the jazz in cozy spots, long talks at night in one of our rooms and working close together we started to feel something towards one another. It just hit me all of a sudden that I actually liked this man. I couldn't let myself go there. I was married and he was married. We were both heading for divorce court. This potential relationship would be a total disaster. Well that was what my head was telling me but usually in matters of love my heart takes over, kicks into full gear and gets me into trouble.

A couple of nights before I was to leave Oklahoma, I get a strange call. The female voice on the other end said, "Why don't you leave us alone. He don't want you?" I was confused I was thinking oh my god Percy's wife. The voice continued, "You done went and put the house up for sale, now we don't have a place for us and our unborn son. Leave us the hell alone!" Click. The phone went dead. Did she say unborn son? Did she say they wouldn't have a house to live in? Who was that ho? I know these dreams have been haunting me for years about Samuel and another woman but this is crazy.

I was too afraid to call Samuel to find out what was going on. Part of me didn't want to know if he really had a baby on the way especially after he denied me the opportunity to have a child. He claimed I would get too fat. Part of me already knew the truth. I was devastated.

I was crying so hard I barely heard the phone ringing. "Hello" I said trying to sound as if everything was ok.

"Jasmine, are you ok?" I heard Percy say.

"I'm. I'm ok. I just..." I couldn't get it out before the tears came rushing out.

"I'll be there in a second."

Percy was at my room in record time. "Jasmine, what's wrong? What happened?"

Between sobs I told him about the phone call. I told him I suspected something like this was going on because Samuel refused to move to Atlanta with me. He just held me and let me cry on his shoulder. He kept telling me that everything would be ok. I cried for what seemed like hours on his shoulder. He didn't rush me.

He let me get it all out. We fell asleep just holding each other.

The next day I apologized profusely. I couldn't believe I broke down like that. Percy was so sweet. He told me even the strongest person needs to break down sometimes. Those encouraging words made me feel a whole lot better but sad at the same time. All I kept thinking about was how can one man be devil and another saint. I couldn't really remember the rest of the trip. I was like a zombie.

Sitting back at my desk in Atlanta, I was daydreaming. I wanted to just throw caution to the wind, get in my car and ride into the sunset. I didn't want to think about my broken relationship with Samuel. I missed Percy. My phone snapped me back to reality.

"Well hello there." Percy, my heart skipped a beat when I heard his voice.

"Hey!" I said as I instantly perked up.

"I was just thinking about you and wanted to make sure you were ok. So how have you been?"

"I have my good days and my bad ones. But my day today just got better now that I heard from you."

"Really! You must have missed me." He said. I could tell he was smiling.

His genuine concern was refreshing. He also revealed to me that he was moving to Atlanta. He said that his wife wanted to be closer to her family. They all lived in Atlanta.

He felt that since they were moving to Atlanta it was definitely the end of their relationship. I asked him how he felt about that and he said that he wanted to keep the family together for the sake of his kids only.

I didn't know how to take that. Can I really be happy someone's marriage is coming to an end? I had to shake that awful thought off. It was bad enough I was heading for divorce court; I didn't want to see anyone else go there as well.

I was working so hard trying not to think about my gloomy life that I didn't take time for myself. So on Friday night, instead of hanging out with my girls I grabbed some wine, a video and ordered a pizza. I went home for some much needed R and R.

As soon as I settle down on my couch with my down comforter the remote in my hands the phone rings.

I ignore it. Then my cell phone rings. I knew it was a sign that something's wrong. I panic because I thought that something could be wrong back home. I ran to grab the phone.

"Hello". I say in a rush.

"Hey, what are you doing?" The voice on the other end of the phone said.

"Percy?" I say. I wasn't really sure if that was him. His voice sounded so different.

"Yeah."

"Are you ok?" I asked.
He started to choke up. "Yes." He said, but I could hear the tears in his voice.

"What's wrong?" I say softening up a bit.

"I don't want to talk about it." He said fighting back the obvious sobs that were trying to escape.

"Come on sweetie talk to me. We've always been able to talk to each other. You have been here for me so I want to be there for you."

"I don't want to talk about it over the phone."

"You're welcome to come over. I just opened a bottle of wine. We can talk or we can watch the movie I got. It's up to you. Maybe it will take your mind off your troubles."

"Ok I will be there in a half an hour."

When Percy got to my house he seemed to be in good spirits. We watched the movie for a while and then he decided to open up. "My wife served me with divorce papers at work today," He said.

"Oh, I am so sorry to hear that." I was truly sorry to see that he was so torn up about this but I still wasn't sure how I felt about the break up. I was growing very fond of him.

"She's moving out. She already found a place." I just listened as he continued to bare his soul.

"This seems so sudden. She didn't say she was this unhappy. I thought that we would at least try for the kids, you know?"

"Do you really think that would be wise if you guys are not getting along?"

"Well, I guess that's not even an option now, so it's a mute point." He said as if he was mad at me as if I was the sole representative of women who broke men's hearts.

"I guess so. Well I'm going to take a shower and go to bed. You are welcome to the couch. Extra blankets are in the upstairs hall closet." I went upstairs and left Percy to his thoughts. I was kind of pissed. He didn't have to snap at me. I'm not the one who's divorcing him!

This shower felt so good. The hot water was hitting all my aches and pains. The stress was seeping out of my body at record speed. I can't wait to drop into my bed. I walked out of the bathroom wearing just a towel, dripping wet. Heading to the bedroom, I ran smack into Percy. He was just standing there kind of in a daze.

"Oh", I said wrapping the towel tighter around me.

"I'm sorry. I couldn't find the blankets. I didn't want to go home to an empty house so I was going to take you up on your offer." He said meekly.

"There in here." I headed to the hall closet.

"Here let me help you dry off."

He walks up behind me as I reach up to get the blankets out of the closets and takes the towel's edges. He starts to slowly dry my back and my hair. I gasped. He removed the towel and started to pat the water from my legs and butt. It felt so good. He turned me around.

He started drying my front. Tenderly he massaged my breast. He then went to my stomach and lingered at my belly button. He went down to my center. He dropped the towel and started messaging me some more all the while staring deeply into my eyes daring me to look away. He led me to the bedroom. He made love to me slowly with so much compassion. The passion erupted in the both of us so fiercely that we didn't know what hit us. I felt an instant connection. It was strange being made love to as if it was the last time. He made me feel as though I was the only woman on earth that mattered to him.

Early the next morning he kissed me goodbye gently and left quietly. I laid there in a daze. What just happened? What am I doing? This is not a good situation to be in. I felt good but I was also miserable. I liked him and wanted to be with him and that made me feel horrible. Also the fact that I just slept with a married man made me feel like a lowlife.

I felt even worse after three days and I didn't hear one word from Percy. I was feeling used. Every time I am feeling blue I go shopping. After work I headed to

Lennox Mall. I was getting my shopping fix on when low and behold I ran into Percy, his wife and their two boys.

"Oh, Hello", I say startled.

"Hi, how are you? He replied very professional like. It was so unlike the man that made passionate love to me three days ago.

"Is this your family?" I say in the best chipper voice I could muster.

"Yes, this is my wife Tonya and my sons Lorenzo and Brandon." He turns to his wife and says, "This is Jasmine. I work with her."

I flashed my fake smile. "Hello." I said. "Well let me let you guys get back to your shopping because I have tons more to do."

Hurt and angry I turn and walk away. I headed straight for the door. Shopping wasn't going to make me feel any better. I was so humiliated. Did I just see that? They looked like a happy little family. Did he make up that story the other night? If so, how could he do something so horrible? Frustrated and confused I went home.

I got home, poured a glass of wine and got straight into bed. I flicked through the TV channels for a while then turned it off. I tossed and turned. I couldn't believe he played me like that. He could have just told me he wanted to sleep me and let me make the decision. In the midst of my mental battle the phone rings. I looked over at the caller I.D. It was Percy. I didn't answer it. My cell phone rings. I didn't answer it. I listened to the messages he sent me.

> *Jas I know what you are thinking. We just got together to take the boys shopping. They needed a few things. We also needed to talk some things over. I didn't call you because I didn't know what to say. I didn't anticipate what happened between us was going to happen and I didn't know how to handle it I am so confused right now. Please call me back. I have grown to care for you very much. I'm sorry for not calling, but please give me a chance to explain in person.*

I was trying to be hard so I didn't call him back. I wanted to so bad but I didn't. I didn't want to go down that road again. I don't want to fall for someone who doesn't want anything from me but sex. I should have known better. I should have seen the signs.

The next day at work Percy was sitting at my desk waiting for me. He handed me a Caramel Macchiato Grande from Starbucks, my favorite.

"I thought you might like this." He said in a soft whisper.

"Thanks." I said void of emotion.

"Look, can I take you to lunch today so we can talk about this?"

"Sure." I said. I would have agreed to anything just to get him away from me and to keep me from looking into his hypnotic eyes.

We went to lunch. Of course it was a quaint dark romantic place. He started talking but my mind was elsewhere. I was thinking of Samuel and how we started with sex and how we ended up. I knew better. I knew that I shouldn't have been intimate with Percy.

"Jasmine are you listening to me?"

"Sorry, I was just thinking."

"Thinking about what?"

"That last week was a huge mistake."

"I don't think it was a mistake, I like to think of it as the wrong timing."

"The wrong timing, meaning that I just screwed you because my wife made me mad and now that we are back together, so sad too bad for you?"

"For your information, my wife and I are not back together. We just needed to get the boys some things. I didn't mean to hurt you last week. I feel such a connection to you. I enjoy being with you. Please don't cut me off. Sometimes just talking to you gets me through my days."

I was torn up inside. Samuel never needed me. He never put his heart on the table like Percy just did. I was melting. I hated to admit it but I was already gone. The funny thing about me is I fall in love quickly. I let my heart take over and I don't think about the consequences. "I am glad to be of service. I always try to help." I said and smiled. Percy loosened up.

"Well" he said, "I'm really and truly sorry. I didn't mean to hurt you."

"Apology accepted." I said as an evil foreboding settled about me.

"So can I come over tonight?" He said slyly.

"Sure I said as long as you are cooking."

The next few weeks were wonderful. It was nice having a man in my life again. We had awesome sex and powerful conversations.

"Hey the company is sending me to Huntsville for three weeks." He said one day

"Oh really when do you leave?"

"Day after tomorrow."

"Wow, I'm getting sad. I just got used to you being around. I am going to miss you."

"I'm going to miss you too? I will be there for three weeks. It's only a three hours drive. Why don't you drive up on the weekend?"

"That's a great idea. I need a little break. I could use a mini vacation."

"Have you ever been to Huntsville, Alabama?

"No."

"Well it's no vacation spot, but I am sure we can find something to do." He said as he grabbed me and pulled me close to him in a bear hug.

Percy called me on Thursday evening making sure I was still coming. He was so excited and his excitement was contagious. He asked me to wear this cute green mini dress that I have. He claims to have big plans for me in that dress.

I got there and I was giddy as a schoolgirl. He made dinner plans. It was a neat little steak house. The lights were dim. We were in the corner secluded. I had my green mini dress on with no panties. Percy was caressing my thighs underneath the table. I could barely get through dinner. I was incredibly turned on. I could have done it at the moment on top of the table.

We finally left the restaurant. We were riding around in a big oversized town car. The rental company was out of mid-sized cars.

"I feel like a pimp riding around in this big ass car." Percy said.

"You look like one with that brim on." I said playfully.

"So I guess that would make you my hoe." He laughed

"Nah nah baby I am too classy to be a hoe, I am a high class escort." I laughed.

We were driving around trying to find something to do when Percy said, "Make love to me?"

"Where are you going to stop somewhere?" I replied

"No, while I'm driving."

"What?"

"Yeah I think that would be a rush. You don't have any panties on right?"

"Right."

"So straddle me."

"But you're driving." I gasped.

"Yeah come on straddle me."

I straddle him and he eases himself inside of me. My body was so ready and willing. He was driving slowly down this darkened street. He was grinding me slowly and passionately. I got so lost in his rhythm I forgot we were actually in a moving car. It was explosive!

That was one of the best weekends in my life. Percy was so attentive and loving. He wined and dined me the entire time. I felt like a princess truly loved. I was floating on cloud nine when I got back home. "Yes I could get use to him being around. I am so happy. I feel like the luckiest woman alive." I said to myself Sunday night alone in bed.

When Percy got back, he didn't call me to let me know he was here. I just happened to dial his number because I had not heard from him in a couple of days.

"Hey you're home. You didn't call me."

"I know, sorry I was busy."

Busy, I said to myself. I was crushed that he just brushed me off that way.

"Oh." I said. "We just had such a great time in Huntsville that I thought it would just carry over."

"I'm glad you had a great time. I had a great time as well. I just have a lot on my mind with my impeding divorce."

"Hmm. So what's going on with that?"

"Well just a lot. I really don't want to talk about it right now."

"Ok, well I got to go. I will talk to you later." I hung up with a heavy heart. I couldn't figure out what was going on. Maybe he is just overwhelmed. I put it out of my mind and tried to stay optimistic.

After that conversation, I hadn't heard from Percy all week. I couldn't bear it any more so I called his apartment. A woman answered the phone. I panicked. I didn't know what to do so I hung up. May be that was the wrong number. I called Percy's cell phone. He answered in a whisper.

"Hey." He whispered.

"Hey, I haven't heard from you in a while. Did I do something wrong?"

"No, I've just been tied up. Hey how about we do dinner tonight."

"Um ok what time?"

"I will pick you up around 7:30. I got to go now but I will see you later ok."

"Ok, see you later." That was strange. It seemed as though he was trying to rush me off the phone. But I let that slide. I was just happy to be seeing Percy again.

I got all dolled up in this jazzy little number I bought last week. Of course it was easy access. Percy was on time. I was surprised at that. He's usually running late. That should have been a forewarning of what was to come.

We went to a nice little out of the way cozy restaurant. It was Cajun. It was quaint. I felt all tingly inside like I was on a first date.

"How are you?" He said. He looked at me with tired, worried eyes.

"Fine." I said. Just a little worried about you.

"I have been hanging in there. I know you want to know what's going on especially after we had such a great time in Huntsville."

"Yes, it would be nice to know what's happening."

"Well, this is just so hard to say."

My heart stopped when he said this. I managed to squeak out "Please, just tell me what you need to tell me."

He looked at me with tears in his eyes and said, "My wife and I have decided to stay together for the sake of the kids."

"Oh" I said as my heart sunk. I looked away. I couldn't breathe. All I could think of was the fact that I was being rejected again.

"Talk to me. What are you feeling? What are you thinking?"

"Excuse me." I said getting up.

"Where are you going?" He said concerned.

"To the ladies room."

I had to get away from the table. I needed a few moments to think. I didn't want him to see my tears. I got into the bathroom and all sorts of thoughts were swirling through my mind. I felt sad, abandoned, lonely and lost. My heart cracked with each tear that fell. I couldn't help but think that his marriage really wasn't in jeopardy. He just wanted to sleep with me. I felt used. I couldn't say anything because I knew the rules of the game. Technically he was still married and I wasn't a factor in that equation. I knew I had to go back out there so I dried my eyes and went back to the table.

"Are you ok?" Percy asked me.

"Yes." I said. "So when did you two decide to stay together, before we went to Huntsville or after?" I said sarcastically.

"Come on Jas. I am not like that."

"Really now, did you think about me at all?"

"Yes that is why this is so hard. I like you a lot and thought this was the beginning of something nice and exciting. However, I have an obligation to my family. Now we can still see each other and have a little fun." He said with a laugh. I wasn't sure if he was serious or joking.

"What" I said indignantly.

"Calm down. I'm just kidding." He said quickly.

"I guess this means we are over." I said. He didn't respond. We ate are meals in silence.

He dropped me off at home. I got out of the car quickly. He got out as well. While I was trying to unlock my door he came up behind me and hugged me. "I'm sorry if I hurt you." He said. I nodded and went inside.

I went upstairs, changed out of my clothes and got into bed. I pulled the covers over my head. I wanted to make the world go away and disappear into never

never land. I didn't want to exist anymore. My phone rings. I look at the caller id it was Percy on his cell phone. He probably wanted to call me before he gets home to his wife. I let it ring. He called back. I turned the ringer off. I just wanted to forget that this ever happened.

I hate weekends. It reminds me of how lonely I really am. I was so excited when I got married. I thought there would be endless weekends spent together. I thought we would explore new territories together. I was robbed of that experience with Samuel. I thought that I would get the chance to have a real relationship with Percy. I was naive.

I was letting my mind run wild with ideas of Percy and his family enjoying the weekend and having fun while I was sitting alone in a three-bed room home with no one to share it with.

"Damn Monday morning. I don't want to go to work." I said to myself as I lay in my bed staring at my alarm clock knowing that it will go off in an hour. "Is that my door? Damn I didn't get my key back from Percy when he came in here last month to re-do my closets." I listened to him come up the stairs. I heard him call my name. I didn't answer. I was hoping he would just go away. He walked into my bedroom.

"Are you alright?" He asked me. "I called you all weekend to make sure you were ok and you didn't return any of my calls." I responded by putting my covers over my head.

"Hey talk to me." He whined.

"About what?" I said.

"Your feelings, about what you're thinking?" He replied.

"Obviously they don't matter. Leave my key and go."

"Look my family is important to me."

"Then what are you doing here? Go, be with them and leave me alone."

"Your attitude is starting to get on my nerves." He said as he jumps on top of me in the bed. "Hmm this is a good position to have you in. Let's have a quickie."

"Get off of me." I yelled. "Get the fuck off of me. This is not funny."

He got this funny look on his face. It was sort of twisted and sinister. He wouldn't get off of me. I tried to raise my hand to move him off of me. He then pinned my arms above my head with one hand and unzipped his pants with the other.

"Let go of me I yelled. I don't want you. I don't want to have sex with you. Get off of me."

"Come on you know you want it. You know you want me. Just a quickie to say good-bye. We didn't get to say good bye properly." At that point he forced himself inside of me. It hurt. I was dry. He tried to kiss me. I turned my head. I kept saying, "Get off of me!" He wouldn't stop. My alarm clock went off.

"Are you going to let me turn that off so we can continue?" He asked me.

"Get off of me." I hissed. He continued to rape me. He didn't get up until he came. He went to take a shower like he did nothing wrong. I grabbed my robe went downstairs, curled up on my couch and cried. I called my job and told them I wasn't coming in today. Percy over heard me call in.

"What, you're not going to work today? Why?" He asked.

"You know what you did." I said.

"I didn't do anything you didn't want me to do."

"I said no. You raped me." He sat there and looked at me. The realization of the situation settled in and you could tell he was wrestling with it trying to make sense of it. He knew what he did but I could tell he really didn't comprehend the magnitude of his actions.

"I did not." He said somewhat dejected. He got up to leave. I curled up into the fetal position and cried.

The next few days were a blur for me. I walked around in a daze trying to forget what happened. In fact I pushed it totally out of my mind. I told myself that I was mistaken, that I really wasn't raped, and that I wanted it.

Percy didn't help matters at all either. He was so nice and generous to me. He took me to lunch several times. He told me that he really wanted to be with me and that he loved me and needed me. He told me I was the only one he could talk to about his problems. He thanked me for being there for him. I believed him. I let myself be taken in by the lies and deceit. I wanted to feel clean again. I wanted to feel needed and whole again.

I let him back in to numb the pain and the shame of it all. I ignored my feelings and let him back in. I let him use me my body just to feel again. We became lovers of convenience. Both trying to force out a dull aching pain of a life we didn't ask for but got any way. I lost my soul in this man. I made myself believe he was my savior of a life I didn't deserve. I gave up me and gave into him, giving him my all. I began to live life as a shell of my former self.

His wife finally left him after six months of trying to make a marriage work that should have never been in the first place. He called me and I could hear the devastation in his voice. He wanted me to console him. I did. We got lost in each other's arms as if this world did not exist.

A couple of weeks later he told me he was moving to Louisiana to take a job promotion and to cut his frequent traveling. I was heartbroken. I don't know why. I knew this relationship was not healthy. He explained to me that this would help him get custody of his boys. He told me that his wife was a cocaine addict and that the boys were suffering on top of that. He said that she helps finance her habit by staring in porn movies. My head was swimming. I couldn't believe any of this. It sounded like a bad Lifetime TV movie.

I consoled him and let him go. Our last evening together was romantic but sad. I cried all the while we were making love. He promised that he loved me and that he wanted me to move to Louisiana as soon as I could. He cried after he said that. I thought he was really sincere. The next day the movers came. He was gone.

The Hospital

I had to stop. I was choking, trying to hold back the sobs stuck in the back of my throat. With every word I was uttering it came out as a primal cry.

Joy came over to my bed, handed me a Kleenex and held my hand awkwardly. She was not used to showing this kind of affection towards another woman. I felt bad. I couldn't help wondering what god awful thing happened to her. She was so cold and distant. She tried to be mean but I could tell that she was a soft and nurturing underneath that tough exterior. I had to know. I needed the focus off of me. I needed her to talk for a while so I can regroup. Besides, I needed to understand her. I felt compelled to try to help this woman.

"What was your mother really like?" I asked suddenly I needed to get her to open up some more. I wanted some type of connection. I desperately needed to feel something. I wanted to feel like I was helping someone so I wouldn't feel like a failure.

The question took Joy by surprise. By the pained look on her face she wasn't sure how to answer that question or if she even wanted to. Her eyes were saying what else a hoe could be like. But I knew there must have been so much more to this woman she called mamma. She had so much contempt for her.

"Well?"

"She was alright. You know, I mean she was ok in the beginning. Being the middle daughter between two sisters, I was neglected a lot, especially after the boys came. She had two sets of twin boys back to back."

Wow I thought to myself. We are more alike than I thought. I was a middle child.

"I'm not sure she even liked me or had time to even like me. It was a total of eight of us," She continued. "She always made me do everything. I was the one that got all of the beatings. I finally just tried to stay out of her way. I retreated into myself, into my writing. My older sister was always mean. She always hit me for no reason, just because she could. I didn't know how to defend myself. I didn't know how to fight back. I was glad when she left even though the responsibility of taking care of my younger brothers and sister fell on me.

My mother beat me as well I thought to myself. Joy continued, "If I didn't do something fast enough, if the kids cried or just if I was in the room, no special reason, I got beat. I never understood why. I was so quiet. I tried to do everything Mamma wanted me to do so she would love me. I was a good girl."

Joy became very quiet. She had this far off look in her eye. I couldn't tell if it was a look of content or a look of disgust. Maybe it was both.

Joy

"Mommy I love you," Joy said.

"I love you to darling." Mommy said.

"Can we play dress up?"

"Sure, what do you want to be today?" She asked gently.

"A princess, living in a big ole' castle with a tower." Mamma came over and bear hugged Joy tickling her until she cried big happy tears.

I used to love those special times we had, before all the others came. My mommy would let me help her get dressed when she was going out. She would dress me up too. We'd play dress up. I would pretend that I was just as pretty as Mamma even though I knew I wasn't.

"Joy you listen to me real good. You just a plain girl. No man is ever going to look at you cause you pretty," Mamma would say. "So you have to be real smart. You smart you know. Always got your head in them books. You keep it that way." She got this far off angry look in her eye when she said that. I would start to cry.

"Hush baby, Mamma just wished she kept her head in them books and her legs closed." Back then I really didn't know what she meant. I do now. When my little sister came it was over for me. She was the darling baby. She was mixed with what I don't know but she had long cascading hair. Pretty smooth light caramel skin and beautiful hazel brown eyes. I was no longer the baby, no longer Mamma's darling.

Mommy never looked at me the same. Mommy would remind me how much more beautiful baby sister was. Mommy loved my baby sister's daddy so much. Drisco was his name. It sounded a lot like Crisco to me. I remember the day he moved in. Mamma quit her job at the post office.

He was something to look at. Drisco was what you call fine with a capital F. He had wavy hair, the good kind not the created kind. He had them hazel eyes too. They even twinkled when he smiled. Mamma would say them eyes is what made her fall in love. He even had a smooth baritone voice that commanded attention.

She was completely smitten. They met at the post office. She told me the story so many times when she cried at night

"Girl what a pretty young thing like you killing yourself working this white man's job like this" He said to her.

"Well seems to me you mo' white then black," Mamma sassed back.

"Is that right?" he laughed

"Yeah that's right and besides I got me two girls at home that need food in they belly and clothes on they back. That stuff 's not free."

"Well look a hear, looks like you need a man to take care of you. Give you all the thangs you need and even some of the finer thangs in life".

"Who might that be?" Mommy said coyly, not believing one iota of this man's bullshit but playing along anyway.

"Now who's standing in front of you right now? I'm all the man you need to wash away all your worries and fears. I am the guy who will protect you from the boogieman. I am the man who will take care of you for the rest of you' life." Drisco said with such intensity that it sounded for real. That was all she wrote. Mamma was in love.

Two weeks later Drisco was a member of our household. He was paying all the bills. I never really knew what he did back then, but whatever it was it was a night. He was a slickster. He smelled of cologne and sex all the time. I believe my mother thought he was some important businessman. He flashed a lot of cash her way all the time. He came to her rescue like he was the Negro superman or something, paying all the bills and putting food on the table.

He was always vulgar with my mother, always talking to her like she was a cheap whore. One night I heard them making love but to my five year old mind it sounded like a fight. I slipped out of bed in my baby doll pj's to see what was happing to my Mommy.

"Come here bitch. Let me at that good stuff you been teasing me with all night."

"Ok daddy. You know the drill though. Pussy ain't free."

I saw him throwing cash at her as she was slow dragging to one of her favorite songs. The next morning he was sitting at the breakfast table.

"Mommy." I called out to her trying to wipe the sleep out of my eyes to focus. She was fixing breakfast. He was sitting there in his boxers. I was in my pj's. He was gawking at me as if he wanted to devour me. I started to cry.

"Shh baby. No need to be afraid of big daddy. He's going to take care of us. He will be here for a while."

She said ever so sweetly. To my five year old ears, I thought she said don't be afraid of your daddy, being as I never knew who my daddy was I assumed this man was my daddy and finally came back for me.

He called out to me. I came to him. He put me in his lap while Mommy fixed breakfast. He rubbed my back and told me not to cry. I liked how he made me feel safe. I leaned back on his chest and fell back to sleep.

That's how it started With him rubbing my back and then caressing my leg. I thought he loved me like a father loved his daughter. I didn't know he wanted to fuck me like he fucked my mother.

He would come home early mornings when me and Sissy was getting ready for school. Mommy worried about that. She didn't have the nerve to ask him what he was doing. She thought it was another woman so she did the only thing she knew how to do. Mommy threw her pills away. "Shh, keep this a secret Joy. I'm a make sure this one sticks around." Next thing I know she was pregnant.

She thought he would marry her when she told him she was pregnant. He didn't. He started paying more attention to me and Sissy.

"Joy you so smart. Show your Mommy what you got on your spelling test. I bet she can't spell half them words you can." He would say goading her.

"Joy get your ass out of here and get ready for school." She yelled. "Sissy you too."

"Sissy before you go, give your papa a big kiss." Drisco grabs Sissy and kisses her on the lips making Mamma angrier.

"She ain't your daughter. This child in my belly is your child. You don't even pay no attention to me and this child."

"Come on now, you know I love you. I take care of you don't I? I put food on the table so you and the baby and the girls can eat don't I? So what's your problem?" He replied grabbing her into his arms kissing her softly. Her tough exterior melted. "Yes daddy, I know you the one that takes care of me." She cooed.

The bigger Mommy got however, the more Drisco's eyes roamed. He would come into me and Sissy's room in the wee hours of the morning rubbing his private part pretending to Mommy that he was just checking on his girls. She ate that kind of shit up. She really felt that she had a good man that wanted to take care of her and her daughters. He didn't.

"Enough about me" she suddenly said, "What happened with you and Rasta"? She was tired of reliving her past. I understood. I was tired as well but the ghost of the past just wouldn't let me go.

I got really quiet. I didn't want to relive it. Think about it. I didn't want it to be real. I didn't want it to have happened to me. I certainly didn't want to bare my soul to her. I didn't want any one to ever know how stupid I was. It's so hard because I knew I needed to get it out. I needed to hear from someone, anyone that I wasn't stupid just in love. I was still so embarrassed. I was smarter then that. I shouldn't have let him make a fool of me and take advantage of me the way he did.

Just thinking about what Percy did to me sent me into an anxiety attack. Hyperventilating, I tried to speak. I couldn't. I ran to the bathroom. I couldn't, couldn't face it. I slumped down onto the floor, curled up in a tiny ball trying to make myself disappear. Joy came in quietly. She sat next to me and just stroked my hair. I cried hard. She cried silently.

With a whisper I began to tell the story of Rasta the awful ending. I recited this poem. The words were inscribed on my heart describing what was left of our happily ever after.

Rasta-Awful Ending
With newfound revelation, I knew with out a doubt he never loved me.
You see, he never asked me to stay.
As we laid there in comfortable silence in each other's arms, my U-Haul packed up loaded down with my entire life in it
He never asked me to stay.
We lay there, three days in a daze lost in emotions, emotions so heavy and so thick thinking about all the times we spent together and all of the times we wasted not being together
He never asked me to stay.
I lay there thinking how much I desperately loved him; how I would do anything for him, how just looking at him made my heart skip a beat –
He never asked me to stay.

I thought about all that I did for him, how I made a fool of myself for him all the money I spent on him, I thought about all of my care and concern for him about the happy life I would spend with him, about the unborn children I would have with him, about the new built from the ground house I would build with him, about the long walks in the park with him, the quiet moments in the house with him the countless Christmases and other holidays with him our golden years together with him- I felt my heart wide open, showing the world how foolish I had been I'd given my life my heart my soul to this man and
He never asked me to stay.

It's hard to believe that someone you love so desperately could hurt you so tremendously. He hurt me beyond any comprehension. The nightmare of my time in Monroe, Louisiana came rushing back to me like the boogieman in a hurry to capture his prey. The nightmare of Percy was always there haunting me....

I was fine a few months after Percy left. He haphazardly asked me every now and then to move to

Monroe, Louisiana. I didn't feel as though he was serious so I haphazardly looked for jobs there.

The last time he was here he talked about this girl Marilyn non-stop. About how she was so nice and kind and how she helped him with the boys when they were there. I kind of looked at him with a raised eyebrow but he assured me she was just a friend. Because of this woman, I felt that Percy wasn't serious about me moving to Monroe.

Since Percy left I became known for having rocking house parties. I was having the time of my life. I had no man to tie me down. He was gone. I was branching out into a business venture and I was making more friends since my company slowed my travel schedule down a bit. Life was good. This particular night, the night of my grand soiree, I had a house full of men and a few of my girlfriends. The men definitely out numbered the women.

Percy came into town for Army reserve duty. He stayed with me. He walked into the house when the party was in full effect. I could tell he was a little agitated from what he saw. After about an hour of me ignoring him and tending to my guest, he called me upstairs to talk.

"Jas, you hardly said two words to me all night. What's going on?" He said in his whiney voice.

"Nothing, I am just tending to my guest. I told you that I was having this party tonight." I answered.

"I know. You told me. You have all these guys here following you around like little puppies. Which one of them are you sleeping with?"

"What are you talking about? I am not sleeping with any of them."

"There's got to be something or should I say someone keeping you from moving to Monroe."

"No, the only thing that is keeping me here is I can't find a job there. Once I find a job, then I can move, besides last week you weren't particularly interested in me. You acted as if you didn't want to be bothered with me." He pulled me close to him and whispered in my ear that he loved me and wanted me to be with him. He was so sweet and sincere. I looked into those hypnotic eyes and fell in love all over again. I resolved right then and there to put more effort into finding a job and moving to Monroe.

Three weeks from that day I found a job in Monroe. I accepted it and was happy to be moving and starting a new life with Percy. I called him to let him know the good news. I just knew he was going to be thrilled. I picked up the phone to call.

"Percy" I said with excitement in my voice.

"Hey" he said as if he was sleep.

"Guess what?"

"What?" he said.

"I'm moving to Monroe. I just accepted a job."

"What? Why didn't you call me before you accepted the job so we could talk about this?"

"Huh" I said. "But we already talked about this. Not just three weeks ago you were standing in my house begging me to move to Monroe with you. What's going on to change that."

"I can't talk about this right now." He said and hung up on me.

My mind was reeling. I just put in my notice to quit my job. My house was on the market and had an offer already. I couldn't believe this. He stood there in my bedroom not three weeks ago and begged me to move and now he can't talk to me. I had to call back to see if this was for real. I dialed his number but the kept ringing. I was devastated.

That night I went to bed early with a heavy heart. I felt so rejected and alone. What was I doing? I knew then that I should have turned down the job and stayed in Atlanta but for some reason my pride wouldn't let me. I was not going to be rejected by another man again. In true stubborn Taurean fashion I forged ahead with the plan to move to Monroe, LA.

Percy called back a few days later to apologize. He told me he was sorry for what he did but I really surprised him. He said everything was happening so fast. He was so vague and indecisive. So I took charge. I told him that everything was already in motion for my move and that every thing will be ok. He will see that it would all work out in the end.

The next few weeks I prepared for my move. I had to go to a training session in Nebraska. I was happy about that because I would be going home. I needed family. I needed to feel welcomed and loved. There is nothing like the sense of comfort that comes over you when you go home. I felt this comfort as I descended the plane at Omaha Epply Airfield.

Training was going well then I got a call from my real estate agent. She told me the people who were buying my house lost their financing so my house will have to go back on the market. I was upset but felt that my house will sell quickly. I said a quick prayer and went on with training.

By the afternoon I was feeling a lot better about the situation and then my manager came to me and told me that the company will not be paying for my relocation as they promised. I was crushed. Now I didn't know what to do. I felt that these things could possibly be signs that I made the wrong decision and I should just stay in Atlanta. Later that evening I called Percy for some comfort. I wanted him to put my mind at ease.

"Hey." I said trying to hide the tears in my voice.

"Hey." He said unenthused. He had this anger in his voice as if I did something to him. "So who are you cheating on me with?" He continued.

"What are you talking about?" I responded as my heart sunk into my chest. I so desperately needed a shoulder to lean on.

He went on brow beating me that way for about three hours. I was tired, frustrated and sad. I finally agreed that there was someone else and how sorry I was and that it was only a one-time thing even though that wasn't true. I would have said anything to make him stop beating me up, to make him stop being upset with me. He then told me he hated me and that he will never speak to me again and don't count on him when I move.

This was the perfect ending to my day. I had the rug pulled out from under me three times that day. I was totally lost. I didn't know what to do. I stayed up that night sitting in the window seat naked, raw and exposed just staring out the window at the stars and praying.

I was looking at my life and asking why and how I had made such a wrong turn. I berated myself and told myself how stupid I was for believing in Percy. I cried into the wee hours of the morning. I wasn't going to be able to sleep any way.

The next day we got our assignments. I would be working in Russellville, Arkansas. I wouldn't have to be in Monroe for a while. That was great because my house hadn't sold yet. To make matters worse, I had to fire my real estate agent because she gave me bad information and lied about it. It hurt to have to do that. She was my friend or so I thought.

The next real estate agent was a bitch. She didn't listen to me and wanted to force me to sell my house way under what I wanted to sell it for. I fired her on the spot.

It was six months into it now and I was getting anxious. I moved on to my next assignment in Mountain Home, Arkansas. Nine months later and my house still hadn't sold. I was so frustrated and angry all the time. I became ill. On top of all that Mountain Home was so prejudice that I had to leave. I had to finish my assignments working in a tiny damp hotel room in Monroe LA, alone. It was spring but down south that equates to humidity, humidity, and more humidity.

Monroe was the kind of town where grown men use bicycles as there primary mode of transportation. It was a small dusty town. It had an industrial, blue-collar appeal. One side street still had the original slave row houses on it or at least that is what they looked like to me. The town reeked of poverty.

Monroe had maybe 100,000 people or smaller. It had two major thoroughfares and two major employers, CenturyTel and State Farm Insurance. This city or better yet this town had dusty dirt roads to top off its appeal, although, it did have a beautiful bayou running through it. But the beauty was lost on the countrified farmer-city folk fishing off the bank as if they were on a lake front resort instead of on the side of the road. Yes this town was truly, as we black folks say Kountry with a "K".

There was nothing to do here. I had no one to talk to. Percy wouldn't talk to me. He called himself being mad at me still. He blamed me for everything that was wrong with him, his career and his relationships. It hurt. I ached so badly. I cried daily. Adding to my frustration was the fact that I went to the closing table twice and twice the deal fell through. Depression set in. I got up. I worked my accounts. I ate sometimes. Sometimes I didn't. I went to bed. I did it all over again the next day and the next. I was getting to the point where I wanted to be dead.

It's funny though; the thought of just throwing in the towel and going back to Atlanta never entered my mind. I was determined to make things work in Monroe and with Percy. I didn't want to be considered a failure again.

Percy called me one day. I was shocked. I didn't know what he wanted but I guessed he just wanted sex. He said he just wanted to talk. Parts of me wanted to believe he missed me and wanted to be with me. Being alone was becoming unbearable. I felt like Jack Nicholson in the Shining. The seclusion was turning me crazy.

Just getting that call made me feel as if I wasn't so alone. As far as I was concerned, any contact was good contact. I just craved to be in his arms even if it was a lie. I hated myself for feeling this way, feeling this needy but with all that has happened to me the last nine months I indulged myself the fantasy. I allowed this fantasy to take over. I fantasized that Percy actually loved me and wanted to be with me. I fantasized he was coming back to get me and we would begin our life together in Monroe.

Loneliness can affect you like that. It makes you think and do stupid things. It tricks you into believing what you are doing and thinking is sane and rational. It will have you messed up so bad that you don't realize you are going insane and loosing all of your faculties. I was torn. I really didn't believe he just wanted to come by and talk. I knew what he wanted, but I let him come by any way.

He came to my hotel room. He hugged me. His scent was so welcoming to me. I missed it. "I missed you." He whispered into my ear.

Drip, drip, drip was all I heard. The sound of my heart melting away the icy exterior I intended to have. "I missed you too." I whispered back fighting back the tears of nine months of anguish and desertion. We didn't talk much after that. He knew instinctively what to do. He peeled my clothes off of me. He stared intently into my eyes as if he knew I couldn't resist him. He was right, his gaze was mesmerizing. Suddenly he just stopped.

"What's wrong?" I said.

He replied, "Damn, I just missed this body so much. Let me just look at you for a moment."

I blushed like a school girl. We made love like there was no tomorrow. I have never felt such passion. From the time he lifted me on top of him, my mind went into full blast to the land of ecstasy. We rode each other for what seemed like an eternity. My entire body ached but in a good way. Sheer bliss came over me. Then he was gone.

I lay there and cried. I didn't like the direction my life was headed in. He knew as well as I did, that he was back in my life. I was angry with myself for allowing that to happen. I was angry that I was willing to let my body be used just so I could have some type of feeling again. The worst part was it only made me feel good for a moment and that moment was fleeting. I quickly returned to hurt and pain all over again my constant companions on this game board called life.

We were on talking terms. He was starting to warm up to me. Percy wanted to help me look for houses. One night we were driving through some newly built and partially built homes. They were really nice. We were walking through this ranch. The garage door was open. It was a three-bed room brick house with a fireplace in the living room. For the life of me, I couldn't understand why homes in Louisiana had fireplaces. It's hot as hell here.

    We met back in the garage of the house after doing some individual exploring. The sun had completely gone down. The headlights of his pickup were pointing into the garage to give us light. Percy came up behind me and whispered in my ear "you look nice tonight." I had on this golden yellow sundress. It fit my body like a glove. It came off the shoulders. It was very sexy. Of course I had on a silky thong underneath. He slipped his left hand under my dress while taking his right hand reaching around my around my right shoulder to caress my left breast. I started to moan softly as he was massaging me. I sometimes forget how his fingers can play a magical melody with my body. My moans got louder. "Shh..." he said. "We don't want to wake the neighbors." He covered my mouth with his hand to stifle my moans while starting to make love to me right there in that garage.

    We drove home in silence. He dropped me off at my hotel room. I didn't say a word. I didn't even say good-bye. He watched me go with this tormented look in his eyes. I closed my hotel room door softly and sat on my bed. I stared into space for what seemed like an eternity. Hurting was all my life had become. It was all I knew. Even breathing was hard. I kept asking myself why he didn't love me. Why didn't anyone love me? What was wrong with me?

I stared at the ceiling again trying to count the holes in the tile. Yes I said to myself in a calm voice this is the beginning of insanity. I am officially going insane. Wasn't there a scripture that says something to the effect that God wouldn't put more on you then you can bare? I think he forgot about me. I think he forgot to turn off the spigot of free flowing problems. He must have got busy or something. I cannot bear any more.

He still didn't want me to come over his place or spend any real time with him. We went to dinner a few times but that was all. Two weeks later I was in Texarkana, TX working my next assignment. This assignment was a disaster. Talk about hill bellies that happened to start businesses! I was frustrated to the hilt and my house still hadn't sold.

Thirty days into the assignment, my house finally sold. I was excited. I would finally be able to move get some normalcy back to my life. I drove the two hours from Texarkana to Monroe to sign the closing papers on my house in Monroe. I got to the attorneys office and was met by my agent. She was distraught. "What's wrong?" I asked getting really scared now.

"Jasmine," My agent says with her severe southern drawl. "They didn't close on your house in Atlanta. The buyer had to account for an extra $500 in her checking account. Once that gets straightened out then we can close. They said they tried to call you."

"I know but when I am working in the field my cell phone doesn't work sometimes. Since I knew I was coming down here I worked all morning and then just high tailed it here. I can't believe this. Where's the restroom?" I was almost in tears but I was determined not to let them see me cry. I went into the bathroom and before I could close the stall door, tears flooded out of me. "Lord why is this happening to me. I try to do what you want me to do. I try to be a good Christian. I work hard. I treat people right. What am I doing wrong? Why am I being punished?"

I finally pulled myself somewhat together and went back out there. I asked to use the phone. I called my agent in Atlanta to find out exactly what happened. She explained to me what happened and assured me that the problem would be easily taken care of and not to worry. I couldn't help but worry but I assured her that I wouldn't. I called Percy because I didn't want to go back to that damp lonely hotel alone. Since it was approximately 3 pm, I called him at work. The phone kept ringing. It felt like an eternity before Percy picked up. I was trying hard to hold back the tears.

"Hello this is Percy."

"Hello" I said close to tears.

"Jasmine?" He asked.

"Yes, it's me." I burst out into a sob.

"Baby what's wrong?"

I couldn't control my tears. I tried to tell him what happened through the tears but all he heard was bits and pieces and a whole lot of sobbing in between. Finally he said. "Baby I'm coming to get you. Where are you?" I told him where I was and he said he was on his way. He got there in no time flat. "Get in. We will come back and get your car. You are in no condition to drive." He commanded. I was obedient. I was in no mood to question or complain. He drove me to his apartment. I was a little nervous cause the whole time I had been in Monroe; he never invited me to his place.

I hadn't ever been to his place so I didn't know what to expect. The apartment was quaint. It had a spacious living room/dining room with a fireplace. It had two bedrooms and two bathrooms down a long hall. I walked in, the first thing I saw was a picture of Percy, and some woman hugged up together sitting on his mantle. I gasped. He looked nervous. I walked over to the mantle slowly. I picked up the picture. I studied it as if I was an alien to this planet and never seen a photograph before. He was in a tux standing behind her. She was in some kind of black formal dress. She was huge. She was black. She was ugly. She had that stern mammy look on her face. There was no trace of a smile. I tore my eyes away from the photograph, with tears at the brim of my eyes, and looked at Percy.

"Let's get you in the bed." He said quickly. All I could do was obey. I followed him down the hall to his bedroom. There sat the bed I bought him that he was supposed to repay me for but never did. He undressed me. He handed me a big tee shirt. He pulled back the covers for me to get in. He turned on the TV I bought him last Christmas when he was still in Atlanta. I carried that heavy 27-inch TV up a flight of stairs by myself all to surprise him. "I have some Merlot, do you want some." He was saying to me. All I could think of was that fat, ugly mammy looking woman and him rolling around in the bed I bought him, the bed I am laying in right now, watching the TV I bought him laughing and making love and drinking wine and hugging and making love some more.

I saw the evidence that he was cheating on me but it didn't compute. I didn't want it to compute. My mind had taken so much that day. I just put the covers over my head and tired to will it away. I was in a catatonic state. I lay there staring at the ceiling fan asking myself how things got so far off course. I asked myself who I had offended so much to be put through this torture. Was

I that bad of a person? I wanted to crawl under a rock and just die, give up and not face any of this madness any more.

I lay there in Percy's bed, what was supposed to be our bed and wept silently. I didn't want Percy to hear me. I longed to turn back the hands of time. I longed to be back in Lincoln, Nebraska with Samuel and at least I would be in my own home. That longing hurt even more because Samuel never loved me either. I was his trophy wife. I was just one of the things he collected and admired but never really appreciated. I was just like the big screen TV he bought. He'd play with me for a while and when he got tired of me he'd put me away. I was his China Doll. He would take me off the shelf, dress me up pretty, show me off to his boys and then put me back in my box and on the shelve when he was done. I was a possession to him, nothing more, and nothing less.

I laid there sad beyond sad. I knew that I had to continue to live but at that point I didn't want to. I didn't see any reason to. In a since I was homeless. The man that I loved desperately is messing around on me. I am lonely and in a strange land. What a combination. Good thing Percy wasn't the type of person to have drugs or sleeping pills around. I could really use something like that right about now. I feel so pathetic.

I fell into a restless sleep. I dreamt that I was being chased and I got trapped in this alley. A big black car pulled up. It resembled a hearse. As I was trapped between a huge garbage can and the hearse, a man gets out with a gun with a silencer attached. He aims at me. I scream.

I woke up with a start sweating and trying to catch my breath. I look around. I don't know where I was. Oh, I said to myself. I am at Percy's. This evil spirit seemed to hang in the air almost chocking me. I tried to shake this evil foreboding but couldn't. Percy came rushing in. "Are you all right?" He asked looking very worried.

"Yeah, I just had a bad dream." I say looking dejected.

"Jas, it's going to be all right. Just pick yourself up, dust yourself off, and do it all over again. There are always going to be disappointments in life, but you have to learn to get through them." He said.

I hated when he did that. Didn't he know he was causing some of my major disappointments? Didn't he know I wouldn't be going through this if he had let me stay here, if he really loved me like he said he did? I couldn't help it. I turned over to face the wall. I couldn't look at him anymore. I ached so badly.

The next day I went back to my hotel room. I lay on the bed and stared at the ceiling. I didn't move. I didn't eat. I didn't shower. I just lay there for two days lost.

Percy called several times to see if I was all right. I didn't have the energy to respond. I was so embarrassed. I was so angry with myself for being the bull headed fool that moved out here when the man all but said all he wanted to do was have sex with me. All I could do was pray. I prayed like my life depended on it. I started to feel a little better. I got up, took a shower and started to work again. It felt good to be productive.

A week later my home in Atlanta sold. Hallelujah! I closed on my home in Monroe Friday afternoon. I moved some of my essentials from storage into my house. Ah, home sweet home. It felt so good to have a home again. I lay there on the floor with the moonlight shining through my six-foot windows and thanked God that this ordeal was finally over.

My home was beautiful. It was a spacious three-bedroom two-bath ranch. It had 9-foot ceilings and plenty of windows. The master bathroom had a Whirlpool deep-set tub and matching his and hers vanities. Sadness crept in like the grim reaper. "There is no his though to utilize the vanity." I said to myself. I wiped the lone tear that fell from my face and started to unpack the few boxes that I brought from storage. Tomorrow my furniture and the rest of my stuff from storage will arrive so I had to shake off the sadness so I can clean.

I am pooped. I have a few more boxes in the garage that were too heavy for me to move. I was contemplating my next move when my cell phone rings.

"Hello?" I said, not expecting to hear from anyone.

"Jas this is Percy. Have you moved in all ready?"

"Yes," I said. "However", I continued because I didn't want to be alone, "there are a few things left in the garage that I can't lift."

"Ok, let me change my clothes and I will come over to help. How do I get there?"

I knew I shouldn't have given him my address. I should have cut him off completely but I was lonely, in a place where I didn't know a soul; a place where even God had forsaken. I told him how to get there and I sat there and waited. I knew we would end up having sex. We always do.

When Percy got there I put him to work right away. I had him moving things to the attic for storage. I had him rearrange my furniture several times in hopes of getting him tired so we won't end up in bed. Finally I ran out of things for him to do. He was sweaty. I was sweaty. He was looking at me with those hypnotic eyes as if they were teasing me because they knew I couldn't resist. "Come on let's test out your shower." He says while grabbing my hand. I follow like I was in a trance. We step into my glass shower. The water was steaming hot fogging up the shower glass door. He takes my shower gel and lathers my entire front side.

"Turn around." He demands in a husky voice, a voice I have never heard come from him. He starts to lather my back, slowly going down my body and ample bottom inch by inch as if he was committing every inch of me to memory. Suddenly and ferociously he enters me, whispering in my ear, "I need this, I love this, don't ever take this away from me."

I succumbed to him surrendering myself my soul to selling out to the devil without looking back or at least trying to fight it. I was a goner. He could do anything. At the point of our climax he was full aware of this fact as well. He could do and say anything to me and I would take it. The power was shifted to him in that moment and lost to me forever.

We exited the shower and got into my huge sleigh bed. We sank down into the pillow top mattress and snuggled under the down comforter. We made love over and over again that night. He left me. He didn't stay the night. Empty was what I felt; so empty that the tears could not fall. I hugged my teddy bear for dear life. I needed a life raft. I didn't have one. The only thing I knew how to do was survive. I would get up the next day and it would be business as usual.

For several months we did the dance of being together and him disappearing. I started receiving hang up calls. I confronted Percy on the issue. He stated that it must be Marilyn. He told me she was upset that he didn't want her and that we were together. I asked him why she should be mad since they were only friends. He said that she wanted him and that she was probably trying to break us up.

He kept feeding me that song and dance for another couple of months. Still something wasn't right. He gave me too many vague answers and responses to my questions.

I called my sister for advice. She was very spiritual so I knew it would be sound advice. She told me to call Marilyn. I was torn between calling Marilyn and just trusting Percy. Every time I decided to just trust him I would get a nagging feeling. My sister told me to go with my gut feeling and that sometimes it is better to go to the source. I knew where Marilyn worked so I decided to call her. I didn't know her last name but figured I would give it a try anyway.

"Hello may I speak with Marilyn please?" I said trying to hide my nervousness.

"The supervisor?" She asked in a cheerful voice and I saying to myself that this is not a pleasure call.

"Yes" I replied as the nerves in my stomach intensified.

"Wonderful I will patch you through"

"Hello this is Marilyn."

"Hi, this is Jasmine." I said with as much confidence as I can muster. "I want to talk to you about Percy."

"Oh", she said and got really quiet.

"According to Percy, you are upset that we are together and you are calling my house and hanging up."

"That isn't the case. Percy and I have been together for the last two years and ever since you came into town he has been distant from me and doing a disappearing act."

"Two years?" I asked in shock. Thinking to myself that was the entire time he has been in Monroe.

"Yes, he told me that you were just good friends and that you were crazy."

We met later that day and compared notes. According to Marilyn, she and Percy stated dating a month after he got to Monroe. He was supposed to move in with her but all of a sudden he changed his mind. He told her that I moved to Monroe to be closer to my family. She also told me that she found out Percy was messing with someone else as well. Her name was Amelia.

My head was swimming when I left. I was hysterical by the time I got home. Percy called me five times. I didn't want to answer the phone. By the time he called again I snatched the phone and screamed "What".

"Well gee what's wrong with you?" He said.

"I talked to Marilyn today."

"Really?" He said his voice going up an octave. "What did she have to say?"

I screamed, "Why did you do this to me. Why did you beg me to come out here when you had a girlfriend the entire time? I hate you. I slammed the phone down and turned off the ringers. I turned off my cell phone. I put the covers over my head and cried. I hurt so badly inside that I couldn't catch my breath. Hyperventilating I cried to God to take this pain away. The pain was excruciating. It was like being cut open alive and watching every time the knife sliced your skin open. I was betrayed. I didn't I deserved this. I was a good person. I loved hard. I was a fair person. I treated Percy like a king giving him pedicures and massages. I gave him erotic passionate sex. Why did he treat me this way?

I heard my garage door open. Damn, I forgot he has my garage door opener. Percy walked into my bedroom. He tried to pull the covers from over my head. I wouldn't let go.

"Jas come on talk to me." He whined. His whiny voice was starting to irritate me. I used to think it was cute now it is just annoying.

"I have nothing to say to you," I hissed.

"You're going to let some bitch come between us. After all we have been through together. After all the years we have been together. We at least need to talk about this."

"Talk about what! You have been with this girl the entire time you were here. You lied to me. You begged me to come down here and you knew you were cheating on me with another woman! You accused me of cheating and you knew you were with another woman. Get out of my house!" I yelled.

"First of all I was not with her for two years. Yes I slept with her but it was only twice. She's angry because I don't want her."

"So you cheated on me with her and you lied about it! What about this Amelia girl?" I screamed my voice expressing my distraught.

He looked shocked that I knew about her but just for a fleeting moment. He recovered brilliantly and did not skip a beat. "She is just a friend. She is a new claims representative from Mississippi and I just took her under my wings to show her the ropes." He continued, smoothly and succinctly.

This was way too much for me. I cried and cried. Percy pulled me into his arms. He told me he would never hurt me like that. He told me that he loved me and always loved me. I could not process any more. I just lay in his arms and cried. It was weird. I felt safe yet in danger. I felt lost yet found. I felt angry yet peaceful. In that moment I realized I needed to leave this place and move on. I knew that I had to start over but I didn't know how. So I lie there and let him love me. I let him push himself in me one more time all the while plotting my escape. He thought it was a moment of ecstasy. It was relief. In my mind I finally came to the realization that I needed to get out of this hell and soon. I didn't know consciously when but it was in progress. So I lie there on another plateau and let him love me and feed me lie after lie.

I stayed with him consciously. Subconsciously I knew I had to leave. I continued to walk through life on shear will. My survival techniques kicked in. I knew I needed Percy to leave this place. I continued to love him consciously; unconsciously I despised him.

Thanksgiving was around the corner. My parents were coming to town. Everything was peaceful. Percy led me to believe that I was the only one he was seeing. In that unconscious state I was in, I believed him despite the post cards he received from Marilyn when she was on vacation telling him she loved him. I believed it despite the time I saw him and Amelia at the mall. I went in and out of depression on the conscious level.

If going insane felt like this, then I was definitely losing my mind. I felt hopeless and empowered at the same time. I laughed at myself and cried. I was happy and I was miserable. Nothing seemed right and yet everything seemed crystal clear. I was definitely losing my mind. On one level I knew I didn't want him and that he wasn't the man for me but on another level, I didn't want to be the loser. I didn't want to lose him to someone else. Crazy, I know. I wanted to be a victor in this game. Game, like this where no one could ever be a victor, only losers. What was I thinking, like someone could actually be the victor in this game of emotions.

With this madness setting in, all I could think about was how I could play to win. Then I got a call from Marilyn.

"Hello" I said, irritated from being distracted from my lunacy.

"This is Marilyn." I smiled a wicked smile to myself. "I wanted to ask you a question." She continued.

"Ok."

"Are you still seeing Percy?" She asked timidly

"Yes, as matter of fact he was here last night and we made love all night long." I could hear a tear catch in her throat. I didn't know why I was being intentionally cruel to this woman. She was a victim like me but in the midst of my madness and pain, I didn't care. It was obvious she didn't care about me being with Percy first because she didn't back off.

"No wonder I couldn't reach him. He told me the other day how much he loved me and how he wanted me to be his wife. I just don't get it."

When she made that statement it hurt like hell. He never stated that he wanted me to be his wife. That made me angry.

"Why would he say that? I asked. He was badgering me about it the other day and stating that he should just move in with me so we can save for our future." I said with intentional cruelty knowing full well he said no such thing.

"We should go confront him, he's expecting me." She responded.

I was angry because he continued to lie to me so I went. That was the worse mistake of my life. She went to knock on the door. I was around the corner by the steps so I can see everything. Sure enough he was expecting her. My anger got the best of me. I came around the corner really fast and tried to get into the apartment. He tired to close the door on me but I was too quick. He was a trapped animal that turned on me.

"You fucking yellow bitch." He yelled at me. "What are you doing here?" He continued. He turned to Marilyn and said, "What's going on here. Can't you see that she is trying to break us up? Can't you see this bitch is crazy?"

With this incredulous look on my face, I said, "How could you say this to me? Is this what I get, after giving you six years of my life?"

Now Marilyn had this shocked look on her face. "But you have only been divorced for two years." She said to Percy.

"Yes," I said to her. "Do the math."

"But you told me you never cheated on your wife." She said to him.

"Baby, can't you see what she's doing, let's go to the back room and talk. "She's lying. She's mad and she wants to break us up." He said hugging and kissing on her in front of my face and that made me lose my mind. I charged him. He was protecting her as if I was trying to get to her. He pushed me with one arm I kept coming. He pushed me into the bedpost. I kept coming. He spit in my face. That was the ultimate degradation. I tried to beat the shit out of him. He grabbed me really hard and pushed me into his highboy dresser. That stunned me. But what came next was unbelievable. Bam. A hard right jab to my chin. It sent me flying back into the dresser, hard. Before the tears could form a left hook caught me square between my right eye and cheekbone and another right to the nose. Blood splattered everywhere. I fell. Marilyn screamed.

My anger was more intense then the pain. "Give me my damn garage door opener and you can fuck all the women you want!" You bastard!" He just glared at me; half frightened at what he did and half-angry that he knew I was telling the truth.

I was humiliated enough. I walked out the room to get his keys so I can get my garage door opener out of the car. His keys were on the table. I grabbed them and headed for the truck while he was still in the bedroom trying to console Marilyn. She was in shock that he could do something like that. So was I but my anger got the best of me.

It took me a minute to find the opener. He hid it well. I guess he didn't want his women to find it. I went back to the apartment. The door was locked. I had his key so I was in the process of opening the door. He snatched the door open and looked at me with this look of disgust. "Get out of here." He hissed.

I yelled, "See Marilyn here's my garage door opening that I got out of Percy's truck." He was trying to block her view by shutting the door on my arm. But he had to open the door back to get his keys from me. He snatched them almost pulling my finger off as well. He then pushed me down with such force that I hit the ground hard. My garage door opener flew into one corner of the porch and my cell phone went flying into another corner. I needed my hands to block my fall. I turned to look up at him with tears on the brink of my eyes, just waiting to fall and me trying to will them not to. I didn't want him to see me cry, to see me broken. He looked at me with fear and sorrow combined. He looked like a little boy who had just kicked his dog and felt sorry for doing so because the dog was his best friend. I got up. I limped to my car like that wounded animal to lick my wounds and of course cry.

With my spirit more hurt and broken then my physical body was from the fall, I couldn't bring myself to get in my bed so I changed the sheets for my parents. It was like I was sleepwalking. I finished cooking Thanksgiving dinner. I tried to keep moving so I wouldn't have to think about what happened but the pain in my side and the bruises wouldn't let me. All I could think about was how I was going to explain my black eye. I settled down on the couch and waited for my parents to come. I lay there in silence. It was dark in my house, dark in my life. The darkest it has ever been.

My parents finally called to say they were turning on my street. I opened the garage for them. It was good to see them. I held my feelings in tact. I forced myself not to cry. We sat up and talked for a while. I got them settled in my bedroom and finally the tears started to roll down my face. I couldn't control them. One by one they fell falling in a pool in my lap. The silent tears are the worse. They mean total brokenness total defeat. I was there in the midst of the pit.

At dinner the next day I couldn't eat. My parents asked me what was wrong. I started to cry. I told them a watered down version of what happened. They couldn't believe what happened. They met Percy. He was so sweet to them. He represented the kind of man they wanted to see men with. He was successful, educated and articulate. He was such a contrast from Samuel.

They could see my eye starting to blacken. I was embarrassed. I wanted my dad to rush over there and kick Percy's ass but I knew he couldn't do that. I told them that I would be coming home soon. My mother assured me that it would be ok and that I will always have a home to come home too. The next day they were on their way to Houston to visit my brother. I felt abandoned.

I called my real estate agent that sold me the house. I told her that I wanted to put it on the market. She came over and we did the paper work. She asked if everything was ok. I told her it was, forcing the tears back so I wouldn't cry in front of her.

I called my girlfriend in Dallas. I couldn't stay in Monroe. I had to get out. I spent the rest of the Holiday weekend in Dallas. I went to church that Sunday and I prayed for my life. I prayed for sanity. I prayed this madness would go away. I prayed for a world where there was no hurt, only love. I prayed for some of everything that day. I thanked God for my life. I knew it could have been worse. I could have been beaten so badly that I went to the hospital or better yet dead. I knew he heard me.

I went back home. I was lying in bed trying to stay sane. Percy calls. I didn't answer. He left the message that he was sorry and that he didn't realize that it was Marilyn's idea to go over to his apartment. He said he wanted to see me. I deleted the message. I fell into a deep restless sleep. I kept hearing this ringing. I snatched the phone off the hook. I figured I had better answer it because it could be my family or my friends checking up on me. It was Percy. "Shit." I said to myself.

"Jas please don't hang up. I'm so sorry for what I've done. I didn't mean to hurt you."

I wasn't expecting an apology. It took me off guard. "You hurt me deeply" was all I could muster up to say. The tears were welling up in my eyes again.

"I know. I know. I am so sorry I hurt you like that. I thought you were the one that spearheaded the encounter. I found out from Marilyn that it was her."

"So that gives you the right to put your hands on me?"

"No baby, I want to see you. I need to see you. I want to explain face to face. Can I come over?" He pleaded.

"No." I said with much more force then I intended to. I didn't want him in my house ever again.

"Then meet me at the tennis courts." He said.
I was torn. Parts of me wanted him to look me in the eye to see first hand my hurt my pain so he can own it. I wanted him to look at the woman who was there for him through his divorce, who helped him get on his feet, and who helped him with his custody battle with his kids. I wanted him to look me in the face to see how crushed I was. I wanted him to see the brokenness that he caused. The other part of me just wanted him to leave me the hell

alone. I wanted him to disappear as if he never existed. I wrestled with this. I still desperately loved him. I wanted to believe that he was telling me the truth that he did really love me that he still wanted me. I gave in to my need to be needed and loved.

"Fine." I said after a long pregnant pause. I grabbed a knife and my pepper spray and headed out of the door. I was scared and nervous. I was sad that our six-year relationship was reduced to this. I wiped away a lone tear as I drove the few blocks to the tennis court. I parked under a light. I didn't see him. I was only going to wait five minutes and then leave. I was singing along with Toni Braxton's Another Sad Love Song. He pulls up along side of me. My heart beats faster. I didn't want to roll down the window. I truly believed he was going to hurt me. He mouthed to me to roll down the window. I did.

"Can I come sit next to you inside your truck?" He asked.

"No", I said thinking it would be hard to get him out if need be.

"Well come sit in here with me. I am not going to hurt you." He replied.

I got in his truck. I kept my hand on my pepper spray just in case. I sat close to the passenger door.

"Why are you all the way over there?" he asked.

"I don't trust you." I replied.

"I told you I wasn't going to hurt you. I am so sorry for what I've done. You just don't know how sorry I am. I'm ashamed of what I did to you." He said reaching over to touch me. I jumped back and replied,

"You should be ashamed. I was the one that has been there for you for the last six years and you take some girls side you barely even know. You hurt me beyond belief. I used to believe in black men. Now I think all of you are dogs. None of you are worth shit. I can't believe you spit on me. I can't believe you did that to me." I started to cry. I didn't want to but it hurt so much. He reached over and grabbed my hand. He kisses it as the tears slip down his face. He says over and over again how sorry he was and that if he could take it all back he would. He told me he loved me. He wanted to go back to my house and make love to me. I was crying even harder.

I removed my hand and got out of the truck. I told him I loved him but this was too much for me right now. I got into my truck and went home. I got under my covers and wept. I wanted my tears to wash away the pain from all of my lost loves; of all of loves hurts. I want it to be the balm in Gilead to remove these war scars from my soul.

I would like to say I told Percy to kiss my ass and left him in lost love history. The truth was I was too needy. I was too insecure. I let him back into my life and into my heart, consciously. Unconsciously I knew it wasn't going to work but at the moment I needed to be needed and wanted. That's what happens with low self-esteem. You feel you can't move on because you're not good enough. I was hoping at least the pain would subside by just talking to him and being friendly.

I stepped outside of myself. I was floating in a world where reality was lost in insanity. This was so surreal. I had no conscious idea of what I was doing with Percy. I kept letting him love me and make love to me. However, I continued plotting my escape. I was like Dr.

168

Jekyll and Mr. Hyde. One face showed pure love and affection for Percy. The other face showed pure hatred.

Percy went back to his old tricks. He became comfortable again. He became the confident hunter. He added another lioness to his leer.

I was going through the emotions of life. One thing I didn't do was take my house off the market. After two months of it being on the market people started noticing it again. A few people came by to look at it. I started gathering boxes to move. I knew I had to go one way or the other even though my conscious self wanted to stay here with Percy. My unconscious self went about the business of saving my life and moving out of Monroe for good.

A few months later my home sold. Percy had mixed feelings. He didn't say much. I wasn't sure if he was still seeing the others my unconscious self knew that he was but my conscious self wouldn't let me believe it.

I wasn't glad but I was relieved that my house sold. I was given a week after I closed to move all of my stuff out of the house and vacate. The day came to move my stuff, my life into the U-haul. Percy came to help. I was moving like a zombie. Parts of me didn't want to leave my house. My house was the only good thing about Monroe. I cried inwardly. I didn't want Percy to see my tears.

After we got everything on the truck we went to have lunch and then went back to his place. I stayed there three days more. We were in some sort of daze. We lie in bed together not really talking just making love. Neither one of us wanted to say what was truly on our minds. I wanted him to beg me to stay. He never said a word. I figured if he asked me to stay then he really loved me. I guess he didn't. On that third day I rose and drove my U-haul with my life packed in it out of Monroe, LA forever. Lost and a loser to love again.

Now that it is done and over, I realized that there are several things that I wanted to say to Percy but never did:

I hate you Percy for making me feel unworthy and unlovable. I hate you for allowing me to fall in love with you and you doing just enough to keep me there and then using me for everything I had and gave to you. I hate you because you preyed on me and abused me all for your own selfish gain. You took my innocence, my kindness and horded it and manipulated it to make yourself feel powerful. You took out on me what your ex-wife did to you. You took out on me what your mother was not. You took out on me what your sisters could not give you. Every woman who hurt you; you paid them back through me by mistreating me. I gave you my love unconditionally. I gave you my soul unselfishly. You gave me bitterness, anger and mistrust in return. You were my love, my life my, everything. I take my heart my soul and my love back. You no longer control me. Although I have this hatred in my heart for you I will get past it. But remember this, I will always love you.

I felt good after writing that letter. I knew Percy would never get it but nonetheless I got out some of my pent up feelings. I walked to the sink with the letter and a lighter in hand. I set the letter on fire. I burned Percy out of my life forever.

From Percy I learned several things. The first painful lesson was, you reap what you sow we both were married when we started out, making both of us cheaters. It doesn't matter if my husband was out there cheating or if his wife was out there doing the same thing. We had an obligation to keep our marriage vows sacred. We didn't. I ended up hurt and I am sure on some level he was too.

The second thing I learned was the importance of loving yourself. Although it was a year or two later that I really got it, I got it. Without self-love, you cannot love any one else. Percy also helped me get closer to God. If it hadn't been for the awful things I went through with him, then I would have never learned how to pray. Prayer is essential in everyday life. It gives you a connection to God. God becomes your life support. He carries you when you cannot go any further alone. He comforts you in the twilight hour, telling you all will be ok once you resigned yourself to quit. God is your protector. I learned that no matter what I did with Percy, God still loved me.

The Hospital

Joy sat motionless. You could tell her mind was processing something but what it was I couldn't tell. I was spent. The story of Rasta took a lot out of me. All I wanted to do was run and hide. I guess, in a since that is what I was doing hiding from all the pain. I wanted to tell her how I got here. How I came back to Omaha and just literally hid out. I wanted to tell her about all of the times I lost my mind in one man after the next in hopes of finding some sanity in all of it. But I didn't. I waited for her to process it all. I really wanted her to reveal to me what she was going through; what brought her here. So I remained quiet and patient, rocking back and forth, waiting.

Joy

About an hour later she starts to talk. I didn't recognize the voice. We were the only ones in the room so it had to be her. The voice was coming from somewhere deep inside of her.

"I was sexually abused from the time I was five years old until he got tired of us all and ran away by the man I thought was my father. Turns out he was just my mother's meal ticket. She knew about it though. She didn't do nothing. She was too afraid if she did that he wouldn't pay the bills no more. I was terrified of him. He would come into my room at night and try to smooth talk me. When that wouldn't work he would grab me, beat me and force himself inside of me. That's when I learned to float outside of myself. I figured my mind was the important thing and he couldn't rape my mind. I would think on important things like ending world hunger and making the world a better place for women like me. I would compose my stories and the next day I would write them down. I knew one day I would get out of this hell and make a difference to somebody in this world."

She stopped just like that. She gave me no more words. She simply turned over and went to sleep. I was speechless. I was exposed to verbal abuse and physical abuse growing up but not sexual abuse. I didn't know what to say or how to comfort her. I just let her sleep. I said a prayer of protection for her and one of healing.

After a while she turned over and continued her story as if she was dreaming it and the nightmare was continuing.

Mommy would leave for the grocery store. She was happy she didn't have to pay no baby sitter since Drisco was there. He volunteered to watch my sister and me. I had a nightmare so I got up and went into the living room where Big Daddy was. I was crying.

"What's wrong with Drisco's baby girl?" he asked sweetly.

"I had a dream that the monster's going to come and shoot us all to death." In the hood we didn't have normal monsters that came to eat you up with their big teeth and fur; we had the human kind with brown skin, masculine features and glocks.

"Nothings going to get my baby while I'm here. Come on and lay down here and go back to sleep."

I lay on his chest and went to sleep. I woke up and saw Drisco pulling down his pants masturbating. My baby doll pajama bottoms lay on the floor. He was just looking at me. He didn't touch me so I pretended I was a sleep until he was done.

One morning when I was a sleep in my room I woke up because I heard a stifled scream. Drisco was in the room. His pants were at his ankles and he had Sissy by the hair. He was forcing her to give him oral sex. She was crying so hard. "Drisco don't. I don't know how. Please. Smack right across the left cheek. He hit her with force. "Just put it in your damn mouth and if you bite me again I will hit you harder." Chocking sounds was all I heard next. "Ah that's it. That's it." He came in her mouth, pulled up his pants and started walking out. "If you tell anyone about this I will kill you, Joy and your Mommy." Sissy started to cry. "Shut the hell up. You old enough to know what the hell's going on." He hissed as he slinked out of the room.

I was terrified. I eased the covers over my head. I stuffed my teddy bear's paw into my mouth to stifle the cries. I didn't want him to come back and hurt Sissy or me. I was six then. Sissy was twelve.

Soon after that he forced Sissy to go out with him most nights. She was never the same. She was distant and angry all the time. Mommy was afraid to say anything on account the baby was coming. She didn't have a job and had no way of feeding us let alone another mouth. Mommy was sad all the time. She cried for no reason. I didn't understand. All I wanted was my Mommy back. She would get angry at the drop of a hat striking me for no reason. Just saying I wasn't moving fast enough. She told me it was all my fault. I didn't understand why she felt this way but if Mommy said it was it was. I tried harder to please her. I did everything she asked me to do and then some. I waited on her hand and foot. She still was sad. She still hit me. I began to retreat into my books and into myself.

"Drisco please don't. I'm a good girl." I woke up sweaty. I was so terrified that he would come after me. My nightmares were getting worse. "Mommy, can I sleep with you?" I said in this small pitiful voice.

"You a big girl now. Mamma can barely move with this big belly I got here. What's wrong baby? She finally said after touching the tears on my face. I couldn't say nothing. I was too scared. I just cried. I knew if I told Mommy what happened Sissy would be dead.

Then one day my nightmares turned into reality. "No Drisco, you not supposed to do that." He kept rubbing me telling me to be quiet. He started to put the snake on me. I didn't know what else to call it. I never seen a man's penis before. First rubbing it up and down my leg. First it was squishy and soft. It started to get very hard. I got really scared and started to cry.

"Be quiet or I am going to whip you." He growled. I couldn't though. I was too afraid. I cried harder. He slapped me. I muffled my cries. He pushed the snake inside of me. I screamed. He covered my mouth and kept pushing. I never knew that kind of pain existed. I felt as if I was being split open from the inside out.

When he was done sticky stuff was all over me. All I could think of was all of my blood was coming out of me. He picked me up and carried me to the bathroom. He placed me in the tub. Then I saw it, the red water. I started to cry again. I knew I was dying now it was only a matter of time.

Drisco spoke to me in soft soothing tones. "What's the matter with Daddy's little girl?"

"I'm dying. It hurts. Mommy. What's Mommy going to say when she comes home and I'm dead?" I sobbed.

"Shhh. I'm not going to let you die. Daddy loves you too much. You're safe with me." He cooed. He cleaned me up, put fresh pajamas on me and placed me back in my bed. Before I fell back to sleep he whispered, "Don't tell your Mommy about this or I will let the monsters kill you."

Mommy finally had the baby, a girl. She was the apple of Drisco's eye. For a while there, things got better. Drisco spoiled the baby. He left sissy alone. He paid more attention to Mommy, which made her happier. We were just like a regular family until Sissy got jealous of all the attention the baby was getting from Drisco.

Sissy started picking at the baby making her cry all the time. Drisco would beat her. He then started to send her out at night on her own. Mommy knew what was going on but she said nothing. She didn't want anything to get in the way of her perfect little family, her man. She worshiped him like he was a god or something. That made me sick to see her flutter around the house catering to him like she was some modern day June Cleaver.

To stay close to Drisco Mommy started trickin'. He treated her something bad but to her she as his main bitch. She did any and everything he asked her to do. He finally gave her to his best friend as a whore slave. She stayed most of the time with him.

I took care of my baby sister. Then the boys came, four of them. Two sets of twins and the baby girl. The boys by Drisco's friend and the last one by Drisco's too but he don't claim her.

They just passed Mommy between the two of them like she was a piece of meat. She was too blind or too stupid to see what they were doing to her. Maybe it was just her self-esteem. Maybe she was so ashamed that she couldn't do nothing about it. Who knows?

It was too much for any one person to handle. Sissy couldn't take the madness any more. She met her sugar daddy while she was trickin' on the Boulevard. He told her she didn't have to work that hard for a no good two bit wanna be pimp. He gave her $500 cash just because she was pretty. The next thing I knew, that pretty boy done had my sister working uptown. She didn't mind it though, cause she had better clothes, more money and a nice place to lay her head. So she just up and left us. She acted like she didn't even know us. From that point on Drisco demanded that we forget about her. We acted like she didn't exist.

When Sissy left Drisco came after me more often. I knew what was next but Momma kept insisting that she was enough for him. Momma then got one of her girlfriends who was strung out to work for Drisco so he would leave me alone. One day I heard Drisco yell, "I'm tired of you crack head whores. I'm outta hear. Heading to

Chi-town where I can make some real money." With that, he was gone.

Momma was devastated. She had seven mouths to feed, no man and no money. She walked out. She said she was going to the welfare office to straighten something out with her check. She left a hundred dollars on the counter. Told me to make sure that lasted for food for two weeks. Out the door she bounced. Two weeks went by. We were running out of money.

That's when I went to him. Tommie. I thought I could trust him. She stopped talking abruptly.

I couldn't believe someone who would call her his daughter could rape her repeatedly. She described a lost innocence in her childhood that could never be recaptured. She spoke of countless broken promises of protection that never came. Until she met him, Tommie was her escape. She fell hopelessly in love with him. He was the only one who protected her. He rescued her from her hell at home. She explained that he was much older then she was and that maybe she was looking for a father in him.

Tommie was her one true love. He made her feel special. He took care of her when nobody else would he was her everything, her entire world.

"So how did you deal with the rape?" Joy finally asked. She had enough of reliving her retched past.

I paused for a long time. I really didn't know how to answer that. I looked at her and said. "I didn't. I believe I just tried to put it out of my mind. That didn't work. I think it's one of the biggest reasons I ended up here."

"I so understand. I never dealt with nothing. Now I'm going insane trying to sort out what's real and what's not. I was trying to find out if I made it all up or if it really happened." Joy said.

"You are not making it up. It happened. You're not crazy just like I'm not crazy but after I broke up with Percy you would have thought I lost my natural mind! I was out on the deep end. I dated and slept with a variety of men trying to drown out the pain of Percy, trying to drown out the rape." I blurred love and sex together. He made me feel like a common whore so I acted like one. I proceed to tell her of "Sweet Georgia Brown, Music Man, Militant Mike and Star Gazer.

Sweet Georgia Brown

Blank, Nothing

The words that come to me when I think of you

Oblivious, dark whole or should I say asshole

Those are the words that come to me when I think of you

User, abuser, selfish loser

Cheap bastard, lying faster then the speed of light

Sun up to midnight you hide your true character faking it

Actin' like you making it thinking you big pimping, giving ladies your guilt tripping   solo dad role you hide your lies in

Broke nigga making eight figures so you sayin'

Lies you tellin' to make your punk ass look bigger

Who you think you foolin'

Runnin' around like the black Adonis

All the while you a tore down no good for nothing brotha

Just chillin' lookin to the ladies to help you in your healing

Not a chance stand up and be a man or

Do you need the ladies to help you do that to?

Those are the words that come to me when I think of you

That's what you mean to me

Blank nothing oblivious dark whole or better yet asshole

      Have you ever been so low that when you called out to God in pain you were convinced he didn't hear you because you feel you're not worthy for even Him to help you. I returned to Nebraska broke and broken hearted. No actually I felt as though my heart was ripped out, shredded and burned to make sure that I would never love or feel love again.

      This was the lowest point in my life. I spent a better part of the year hidden in my three-bedroom house in the hood. I figured no one would track me down there. I was in hibernation. I didn't want to see any one. I didn't want to interact with anyone. I just wanted to be left alone to wallow in my own pain.

      I couldn't believe how Percy did me. Didn't I pledge my undying love to him? If it were easier to die, I would have. But it wasn't. I knew I had to live and go on but how. Just as I was feeling like I didn't want to go on any longer Tory my childhood best friend said she wanted me to meet someone. Not that I really wanted too but I was lonely. I was sad all the time. I thought this would be a good time to shake myself out of my funk. It was just supposed to be something to do.

We were sitting at our favorite coffee shop having coffee just catching up and talking about nothing. Her phone rings. It was her personal trainer. He was checking up on her to make sure she was following her diet and workout ritual he prescribed. She mouth's to me "this is him; I want you guys to meet." At that moment he must have asked her who she was with because she told him she was sitting with me. She handed me the phone to talk to him.

"Hello" I said

"How are you?"

"Good and you?"

"So what are you two ladies doing this evening?"

"Just having coffee and talking?"

"Tory asked me to come down, to hang out but I have so much to do with my business that I can't."

"Oh so you can't come down to meet me huh?"

"No not today. So what do you do?"

"I'm a techie. So I understand that you are a personal trainer?"

"Yes and I work in market research"

"Oh market research"

"Don't let that Negro fool you, he's the manager!" Tory chimes in.

"Hmm" thinking to myself, why didn't he just say that?

"So do you want to exchange numbers?"

"No, since you can't come to meet me then you can't have my number?"

"So when do you want to meet?"

"It's up to you, this weekend or next."

"Ok we can meet this weekend, Saturday ok with you?"

"Yes"

"So how will we communicate?"

"You can email me."

"You know I am not really looking to be a in a relationship."

"That makes two of us, me neither."

I gave him my work email address and hung up.

"Girl, why that Negro trying to rap to me and then turn around and say he's not looking for a relationship?"

"You know how men are, they're always looking but don't want to admit it." Tory said.

All sorts of thoughts were running through my mind. Is he going to be just like every other sorry man in my life? Will he know how to treat a lady? Is he secure in himself? *Hold up Jasmine, you are getting ahead of yourself you haven't even met the man yet.*

The next day Alvin emailed me. He called it getting to know me. He asked several questions. He was getting intimate over email. He asked the kind of questions that should have been asked and answered face to face. I didn't mind though. I just got out of a relationship with Percy and it was kind of nice to be seduced slowly. He said all of the right things at the right time. I was so smitten with a man who had some sophistication. He knew all the right restaurants and the right wines. He talked about books and poetry. He talked politics and he had a sense of humor. I didn't stop to pay attention to the signs. I was thinking he is genuinely a nice guy. I liked that. I have never had that in my life.

Although Tory said he was fine I still was a little skeptical. He was also. He kept asking me what I looked like in his emails. I kept giving him the basics, light brown, about 5'4" and average height and weight. Finally he sent me a link to his website so I could see what he looked like. That should have been a sign that he was vain and thought of only himself. I must say though, he looked good but photos never did any one justice. I still wouldn't send him a photo of me or adequately describe myself.

Our Saturday date was approaching fast. He was getting anxious. He suggested I come by his job to meet him. I obliged.

He's a manager of a marketing research firm. I pull up. Nice. The office complex was new. I was impressed. I call him.

"Hello."

"I am outside."

"I'm on my way out."

My heart is racing. My head is saying here we go again. For me, meeting someone new that I was interested in made me a little crazy. This time it's going to be different. I'm going to take my time. Get to know him, especially before I jump into bed.

Oh my God. This Negro is fine! He came walking towards my car. Shit. I dropped my keys. I am trying not to let him see me drool. As he got closer, all I could say was DAMMMN! It must have been a casual day. He had on a gray slightly tight sweater that showed his muscular upper torso. His jeans had a nice fit to where you could tell he had a nice ass. The jeans fit him perfectly; they were not tight or sagging.

He was somewhat short about 5'8. Dark chocolate you know the Hershey's special dark flavor! Bald and clean cut. Just how I like em. I am so glad that he looks like a personal trainer. I hate it when some one doesn't represent their profession well. Like hair stylist whose hair looks like it has seen its last day and they want you to sit up in their chair. That kind of hair stylist can not touch my head.

"Hello"

He hugged me.

"Hello" I said. Umm and he smells good too.

We walk into his office. I guess he wanted to show me that he was the boss. Showboating is what I call it. We chitchat for a while. Nice personality. Good since of humor. I like what I am seeing so far. I leave quickly to reel myself in. I don't want him to think that I was totally digging him. You know how men get. They get the big head when a lady shows her admiration to soon.

Driving home with cell phone in my hand, about to call Tory to thank her for introducing us, this weird feeling hits me. I can't explain it. It just envelopes me as if to say Jasmine, girl watch out, don't do it to yourself again. I ignore it. I love being in love. I love being close to someone. I love getting caught up making someone happy. I just love the notion of love. What can I say, I am a hopeless romantic!

I call Tory/

"Hey Girlie" Tory says.

"Gurrrrl, all I can say is DAMMMMMN, that Negro is fine!

She lets out hearty laugh, "I told you. It is so hard for me to work out with him in the mornings. I have to stare at his fine ass. Literally stare at that tight hard ass he has."

"I know I made him walk in front of me so I could get a good look at it."

"Whew, it is going to be hard for me to restrain myself. I wanted to jump his ass today."

"Girl get your freak on."

We laugh about it a little while and hung up.

Getting undressed for bed that night, that feeling came back, haunting me. Could I be making a mistake by just going out with this guy? Naw it's not like I am trying to marry the man. I just want to go out and have a good time. Percy gave me enough heartache to last a lifetime.

Sadness overtakes me, just thinking about him. I had it all planned out. Percy and I would get married, build a house together and have a baby. Perfect. There wasn't supposed to be two other women in this picture. I went to bed with a heavy heart. I hate starting over. I want love to last.

I cannot believe I am standing here changing my clothes again. It's only a date. I keep telling myself. I finally found an outfit that works. Not too suggestive but just enough to showcase my best assets.

I opted to meet him at the restaurant. I didn't know him. He could have been a serial killer or something. Never hurts to be safe.

The restaurant was nice. We went to an upscale sports bar. It was a trendy place that yuppies frequented. It was dimly lit a kind of cozy place to be a sports bar. We sat in a corner booth. It was perfect, semiprivate so we could interrogate each other as newly joined people do.

"Tell me about your business," I said.

"I am a personal trainer as you know. I don't work for a gym. I believe it is important for my customers to feel comfortable enough to work out hard, so I usually go to them. I put together an exercise program tailored to their physical make up and eating habits."

"Hmmm, interesting" I could tell that he likes to talk about himself. It was cool though. It was nice to see a brother who was trying to do something positive.

"So then do you suggest an eating plan as well?"

"Yes, I try to get them to eat more fruits and vegetables cut out beef, sweets, and sugar things like that. Enough about me, tell me about you? Do you have any kids?"

"No, it is just me. I just moved back to Omaha from Louisiana."

"What part?"

"Monroe"

"Where's that?"

"It's northern Louisiana. It's about 75 miles east of Shreveport."

"Oh ok. How did you get there?"

"Long story."

"In other words code for you don't want to talk about it."

"Yeah, something like that."

"Sounds likes there's a story there but I won't push. So what do you like to do?"

"I like to read. I write a little poetry. I have been expanding my music interest into neo soul, classic Jazz. Not the jazz they do today but Coltrane and Bird"

"Yeah, I like neo soul as well. I dabble in poetry myself."

"Really, you will have to show me some of your work. So you have kids?"

"Yes, I only have one son he's nine. He lives with me?"

"Only one son huh?"

"Yeah"

"Where's his mother?"

"She lives in Valdosta, GA."

"Ok so why do you have your son?"

"Well she wasn't taking care of him properly so I went and got him. It's hard being a single father but I love my son and I want the best for him."

"Wow, I bet it must be hard, but you know little boys do need their fathers. I think it is admirable what you are doing. I wish more fathers would take more interest in their kids." I was thinking wow this guy is awesome. It has been a long time since I have met a man who is sensitive, responsible, and ambitious. I was beginning to really like him. Damn there goes that evil foreboding feeling again. What is that? Can't I just like a guy?

We talked for what seemed like hours. We laughed and teased each other. The conversation flowed easily. Something I haven't had in a long time. It felt good or then again it could have been all the wine I drank either way I was having a good time. We left the restaurant and drove around for a while just talking.

We went back to his place to watch a movie. He had a bottle of Riesling chilling for me. Nice touch I thought. Since he had a roommate and since his son was in the other room we watched the movie in his bedroom. We were snuggling close to each other. I could tell he was a cologne man. He smelled so good. It has been so long since I have been this close to a sexy, good-looking hunk of a man. My insides were raging out of control. I was getting light headed the world was spinning. We were really feeling each other.

The next thing I knew we were kissing deeply passionately. He put his hands underneath my blouse and unsnapped my bra. I didn't stop him. The mantra of it's been so long since I have been held, kissed and made love to was playing a sweet symphony in my head. He pulled my shirt off. He kissed me deeper. He pulled my pants off. Kissed my thighs, slowly making sure he kissed ever inch of my thick caramel thighs, legs and feet. I was a goner then. When a brother sucks my toes something happens inside of me that makes me loose all reason and logic. He slipped a condom on and the next thing I knew he was inside of me. Stroking really fast like he couldn't believe his luck. He slowed down a bit as if he realized he was acting like a sixteen-year old schoolboy doing it for the first time. The sex was ok. Not bad but not great either. I could live with it. He was a nice guy. He seemed ambitious and to have a good head on his shoulder.

After that night we saw each other almost every night. He was so sweet. He would call me at work in the morning just to see how my day was going. I so appreciated this because my job was stressful! If I didn't see him in the evening, he called me to wish me a good night.

"Hello" I said with such nastiness in hopes of giving the person on the other end of the phone a warning as to not mess with me today.

"Baby it's me, Alvin."

"Oh hi, sorry for the attitude."

"Not having a good day?"

"Yeah and it is still morning. I can't wait to see how the rest of my day is going to go!"

"I am sorry to hear you're having a bad day. I tell you what, before you go home today, stop by my office."

"For what?"

"You know how just seeing me makes your day." He said with a laugh.

"Whatever!"

"Seriously, come by, I would love to see your pretty face and give you a hug since you're having a bad day."

"I am only going to get a hug?"

"Yeah in public, but when I get off you better watch out."

"Bye" I said laughing as I hung up.

I drove to his office after work as ordered. I didn't feel like going in so I called from my cell phone.

"Hey I am out here."

"I will be out in a minute."

I was just really irritated. My day went from bad to worse. Why is he taking so long to get out here? I am so ready to go home. I was rubbing my temples with my eyes closed so I didn't see him come out. I jumped at the tap on my window. I rolled it down.

"Get out of the car so I can give you a much needed hug."

I stepped out of the car.

"Here, this is for you."

He handed me a beautiful long stemmed red rose. I was almost in tears. I threw my arms around him and gave him a big hug.

"Thank you, you just made my day."

I went home with a smile on my face. I forgot about my headache. I thought I was special. I finally found a man who was honest, who liked different types of music not just rap, who liked poetry, who was ambitions, and who knew how to treat a woman. I was happy.

We had been dating consistently for the last 30 days. It was wonderful to have someone to hold me at night and to go out with on the weekends. We went and did something every weekend. He even took and washed my clothes. Now how many brothas offer to wash your dirty drawers! I was loving it!

One day we had a conversation about salaries. He told me what he made. Why, I don't know because it really didn't make a difference to me. I was just happy to have someone that had a drive and ambition that matched mine.

"So how much money do you make?" he asked.

"Seventy-five." I said nonchalantly

"Seventy-five thousand dollars?" He asked as his voice went up an octave.

"Yeah" I said wondering why he was so concerned.

"Oh, I just didn't know how much you made."

I changed the subject because I didn't think it was that big of a deal. He dropped it also, so it seemed.

It was getting pretty serious really fast. Alvin and I had a real heart to heart talk. I asked him if he has told me everything about himself because I had some pretty heavy things to tell him about me and my past relationships.

"Are you sure you told me everything? Have you put all of your cards on the table? No skeletons in the closet"

"Baby I told you everything."

"Are you sure?"

"Yes, I told you everything? What is this all about?"

"Well I want to tell you about me and my past relationships. I want to put all my cards on the table. I really like you and I just want everything up front and out in the open."

"Ok"

I didn't know where to start so I started at the beginning. I told him about my relationship with Samuel; how he mistreated me, lied to me and cheated on me. I told him about Percy. I told him that I really loved Percy and that he hurt me to the core by lying to me and cheating on me and giving me Herpes. That was the hardest thing I to do, revealing that to him. He looked at me like I told him I had AIDS. He looked at me as if I was a dirty slut or something. The truth of the matter was I was a faithful wife and a faithful girlfriend and the thanks I got was a disease that I couldn't get rid of.

"I can't believe this. Why didn't you tell me this in the beginning?

"This is the beginning; we have only been dating five weeks?"

"I was falling in love with you, I don't know if I can handle this. I got to go."

I was in shock. Herpes is not some dangerous disease that you could die from. It's cold sores that just happen to be on your genitals instead of your mouth. I watched him walk out the door. I cried that night. I cried for myself and all of the other sisters out there who loved unconditionally and who believed that their men are faithful so they don't protect themselves. I cried for me because I didn't deserve what I got. I cried even harder because I was so naive that I didn't protect myself.

Alvin called me two days later. He told me he was in love with me and that he could live with the herpes. I was relieved. I didn't want this thing to hinder me from a possibility of a great relationship.

Wow! What's happening here? I said to myself one morning. Alvin and his son were living with me. *What am I doing? It's too soon.* My panic attack was taking over me. I looked over at Alvin. He was sleeping so soundly. I got up and went to my big picture window. I liked to talk to God that way. I stood there for what seemed like an eternity. "God, I don't know how I got here. I know this is not right. I feel it deep in my spirit. Not just living together, something here is seriously wrong with this man. He appears to be too perfect. Lord help me. Protect me from evil. Show me the way. Reveal to me his true colors, true character. In Jesus name I pray. Amen."

Three days after I prayed that prayer, I got the shock of my life.

"Good morning this is Jasmine, how may I help you?"

"Hey this is Alvin, I can't believe this, I have something to tell you?"

"What?" I said totally alarmed. He hesitated, pausing for a long time before proceeding.

"I have another son."

"What, What are you talking about?"

"I got the paternity test back and the baby is mine."

"What are you taking about; you said you only had one son?"

"I know, I got the test results back today and I am telling you now."

"I am not following you how old is this child?"

"Two months."

"You have a two month old son and you didn't tell me about this?"

"I just found out today."

"This girl who ever she is just showed up today and said this is your son and you are the father?"

"No see what happened was that she was my ex-girlfriend and we had slept together and the condom broke. I begged her to get an abortion but she wouldn't."

"So then you knew the child was yours and you didn't tell me?"

"No see, I'm trying to explain...

"I can't deal with this right now, I am at work." I disconnected the line as he was asking me to stay on the line and discuss it. On the verge of tears I ran to the bathroom, upstairs away from my office. I didn't want them to see me cry. I can't believe this shit. I lay all my cards on the table and this motherfucker tells me he has another child! I can't believe this, I sob. What the fuck is going on here. He portrays himself as this honest hard working single father just trying to make it. Lies, Lies, Lies. Fuck here I go again. I can't buy a good man!

I was too disoriented to stay at work. I didn't know where I wanted to go or what I wanted to do. I drove around for what seemed like hours, crying and trying to figure out why he didn't level with me. I asked him several times if there was anything else he wanted to tell me. Each time he said no.

Alvin has been blowing up my phone for the last hour now. I guess he called me back at work and they must have told him I left for the day. I just can't face him now. All I can think of was all of the lying men in my past, especially Percy. Men always grumble about how we always want a thug and how we don't give nice men a chance.

Well Alvin claimed he was a nice man trying to do something and not hanging out on the streets but he is just like the rest of them a no good lying motherfucker! Mr. I'm just a single father trying to make it, putting down all these other brothers who father kids and don't take care of them and putting down those who don't practice safe sex. Just a liar. Now I know he told me that the reason he has his older son is because the condom supposedly broke. So now he expects me to believe lighting struck twice!

I finally went home. It was dark just like my mood. I opened the door and walked into a dark cold house.

"Oh, you scared me!" Alvin was sitting on the couch in the dark.

"Can we please talk about this?"

"What's there to talk about? You have another son. That little tidbit if information you failed to mention to me when I asked you three times if there was anything else you needed to tell me. I laid all my cards on the table and told you everything about me so we can have an honest and open relationship and you left out key information. And you treated my like shit for being open with you I might add. Why?"

"I didn't think the child was mine."

"So you basically weren't going to tell me about this?"

"No, if the child wasn't mine, no."

"I see. That would have been the upstanding thing to do. So why did you think the child wasn't yours?"

"Well she was sleeping with another person at the time."

"She was sure?"

"I guess so. She wants me to pay child support so that's why I demanded a paternity test."

"Hmmm"

"Baby, I am sorry I didn't tell you I just really didn't think the child was mine."

"How old is he?"

"Two months."

"Two months!"

"Yes"

"How recent was this relationship? How can you be so in love with me and you have a two-month-old son? The relationship has to have been in the recent past! You led me to believe that you were single for a while."

"We weren't together at the time."

"So it was a booty call?"

"Yes, something like that."

"Do you love this girl?"

"Jasmine, I told you we were not together."

"So what did she think?"

"About what?"

"Did she think you were together?"

"No she didn't. I told her under no circumstances we were together. She wanted to stay together though."

"Hmmm."

"Whose condom was it?"

"Hers.

"Hmmm."

"What?"

"So it seems as though you are telling me that this girl really loved you, she wanted to stay together and then she ends up pregnant?"

"You do the math."

"So you think she trapped me?"

"I don't know but two and two is adding up to five here."

"So what's the child's name?

"He's a junior."

"And you said you didn't know that was your child?" I said with a role of my eyes.

He looked deep in my eyes, "Baby I love you so much. I don't want to lose you."

I didn't believe it but I wish I could say that I was strong. I wish I could say that I wasn't needy and told Alvin to get the hell on, but I wasn't. I so desperately wanted to believe him. After all that Percy put me through, I just wanted to have someone in my life that was genuine and real even if I was deceiving myself. I convinced myself that he was telling the truth. I stayed with him.

Alvin stared deeply into my eyes and asked, "So what are we going to do? I love you."

I stared back, sighed and told him that I loved him too even though in the pit of my stomach I knew he had lied. I lied too. If I were really honest with myself, I would have admitted that I didn't love him. Never did.

I hate birthdays. They remind me of the shit I haven't accomplished yet. This up and coming birthday was no better. I was in a funk. I was getting older. I found out that my man has a two-month-old child. It's hard because I really wanted children. What do you do when your man has two baby's mamas? I don't think I can handle that type of drama!

"Hey baby I know your birthday is coming up. What do you want?" Alvin said breaking my gloomy thoughts.

"I don't know surprise me, be creative." I reply. This usually separates the men from the boys. Boys will get you what they want you to have or what they think you want. A man will take the time to study you, find out your hidden most desires and present you with a gift that satisfies your emotions, thus endearing you to them even more. A man will know just what to get to bring out your very essence and make you love him even more.

"Well I usually like to do things a little different. I will definitely surprise you."

I am lying here in bed willing this day to go away. I am a year older. I lay here contemplating what the fuck I have gotten myself into. Can I really make a life with this man? Who is he anyway? Why am I an instant mother after only a short few months? To top it all off he was the Lay-A-Way King! How cheap is that shit!

"Happy Birthday Baby. Here I brought you your coffee." Here comes that Negro, interrupting my thoughts again.

"Thank you." I say with a forced smile on my face. Damn can I just get one moment of peace with no one talking to me? I am just not the morning person. I just want it quiet in here when I first wake up. Jasmine stop being a bitch. The man brought you coffee for peat's sake! This mental sparring wears me down every time. I soften up and kiss Alvin to show him how much I appreciate him.

"Well see you later and have a good day today." He kisses me and leaves. I am thinking wow; he must have something super duper planed for my birthday because he was surely keeping it under wraps! Maybe he is going to send flowers to my job. No that is too common. He said he does things differently. I am too excited. I finally found someone who thinks outside the box and can be romantic.

I was expecting something great all day. Nothing came at work. *Well something has to be at the house since he works until nine. I just know he left me with something special to come home too.* I say to myself. I open the door. Nothing. I went into the bedroom. Nothing. I went into the kitchen. Nothing. My heart sank. *Well maybe he is going to bring me something when he gets off work.*

I lay down depressed. I closed my eyes. Sleep came. I was in a land where everything was a-ok, where I had a man that surprised me with a weekend trip to Jamaica in which I didn't have to pack a thing, just get on the plane. Let's just go to the airport as is. Everything you will need is there waiting for you. Now that would be a great birthday surprise.

He's here. I heard the car pull up. I pretend to be asleep. He comes in the bedroom. He kisses me. "Happy Birthday" he whispers.

"Thank you." I say.

"I have something for you."

I follow him to the living room. There was a huge balloon and a stuffed lamb waiting for me. *Do I look like a damn child!*

"Thank you." I say. My heart sank. I didn't know what I was expecting but this wasn't it.

"We will go out tomorrow also. What do you want to do?"

"Oh" I say another disappointment. He was supposed to be this romantic thinking outside the box person who had it all under control. I figured that he would have had everything planned. "Dinner and dancing sounds good."

"Ok. Well I have appointments all day so we will just play it by ear tomorrow."

"Play it by ear," I said to myself. "It's my fucking birthday. Play it by ear." All I could do was go to bed. I was in no mood to cuss a Negro out tonight. "Ok", I said. "Well I am going to bed. I am tired." I was broken hearted.

He was just like every other nigga who said what they thought you wanted to hear to get you. I should have left him alone and called it quits early. I knew better. There would be no improvements at this point. But I couldn't. I refused to believe I have been duped again. I thought, I was maybe jumping to conclusions. Maybe I wasn't giving him a chance.

Saturday morning. I woke up to smells of breakfast cooking. I was excited. Breakfast in bed is so romantic. Alvin walks in the room with no tray. He was fully dressed with his coat on ready to leave for his morning appointment. I guess breakfast was out! He asks, "Jasmine can Kenny stay with you this morning? I already cooked him breakfast" Ok I'm thinking to myself, what makes him think I want to baby sit his son on my birthday especially when he didn't bother to fix me breakfast as well? The brotha lost his mind. The nerve! "No" I say. "I have some errands I need to run."

That evening he got home late. I was steaming. He took his sweet time getting ready. He's worse then a woman, primping and prancing in front of the mirror. Making me wonder if he has some sugar in his drawers! Maybe this means he made reservations to some place nice for dinner.

"I'm ready. Where do you want to eat?"

"Um, you didn't make reservations any where? Well I don't know. It's already 10 o'clock. You know everything closes here early. I said with my irritation bursting to come out.

"I know and I still have to take Kenny some clothes and pick up their pizza."

"What?"

"I'm sorry baby but he has to eat."

"Your brother doesn't have food over there?" I said totally irritated!

"Apparently not." He said in an irritated voice. This pissed me off even more. I wanted to say just forget it but I didn't. I know I can be a bitch some times so I just left it alone.

By the time we got done with all of our deliveries it was 11 PM. All restaurants were closing up.

"Everything is closed." I said in a huff.

"I know. I'm sorry. I will do better next year. I just wish I had more time to plan."

"Well how much more time did you need. You had a week. Well next time take two weeks to plan," I said. "Then maybe you will be more organized and things would flow smoother."

He looked at me as if he wanted to kill me. I didn't care. He was the one that said he did things differently. He was the one that told me he was not like the average brother and now I am totally disappointed. I am angry because I believed the bullshit he was telling me.

We ended up going dancing first and we had a great time. Dinner was another story. After driving around for what seems like hours, he pulls in this lonely desolate parking lot and only one business had their lights on. The lights were on at Village Inn. I couldn't believe it. It wasn't even one of the new renovated Village Inn's. It was broken down. It had a shabby dirty awning that sagged to the left.

We walked in. It was dank in there. It sort of smelled like a musty old cellar. I scrunched up my noise trying to get that smell out of it. Village Inn was the lower class version of Denny's. I have never been to Village Inn for my birthday! I was expecting candle light, ambience, a five-course meal not waffles or pancakes! I was highly upset. All in all my birthday was a disaster. What a cheap ass bastard. The Village Inn?

We were approaching six months. Some days were good some days were not so good. I figured that was just life. I was counting the days that his son would be going away for the summer. Don't get me wrong, he was a good kid but he had ADD and that kind of worked my nerves. I was not used to having a child around let a lone one you have to entertain twenty four-seven. I also wanted to take some time to get to know Alvin, one on one.

His son was gone a week. His aunt called to have Alvin come and pick him up. He was just too much for her to handle. I was bothered by that. Alvin worked all day and on the weekends so where did he think Kenny was going to be for the summer. I don't have that kind of experience with kids or the patients.

We went to pick him up. Of course we took my car.

"Alvin, what are you going to do with Kenny for the rest of the summer?"

"I am not sure, he can go to the Y during the day but I would need someone to pick him up from there."

"I don't mind picking him up." I said that thinking I would pick him up and take him to his babysitters until Alvin got home. Little did I know Alvin wanted me to take care of his son for the rest of the evening until he got home.

I was right. Everyday after Kenny went to the YWCA walked to my house. I had to entertain that kid. I would force him to go outside. He was kind of big so he didn't like to go outside to play. He would rather hang out in the house under me asking me every five minutes when's dinner. I got so tired of that shit. I felt bad because I was fond of the little boy but I just thought it was unfair of Alvin to force me to take care of his child. We barely knew each other and now he wants me to take care of his kid. I was starting to wonder if that was his agenda all along and that was the reason he pushed for us to be a couple so quickly. Just thinking about this makes me sad. I feel really stupid. I really wanted to believe he was different. It is turning out that he is just another nigga trying to get over.

I went over my friend Tory's to help me get over my looser boyfriend blues. She always made me smile.

"Tory, I don't think I can take any more of this."

"Why what's happening now?"

"Well not only are we not making love any more, I have his son all the time."

"What?"

"Well he claims that since he's not eating red meat any more he has no sex drive."

"I never heard of that."

"Me neither. To make matters worse I asked him when he stopped eating red meat. He told me eight months ago. Our sex life was fine in the beginning. I'm starting to think he just wanted a baby's Mommy to take care of his son."

"You guys did move kind of fast. Maybe you should take a break. What ever happened with that girl he was always calling in the afternoons when you were at work?"

"He claims she was a personal trainer as well and that they just talk shop. But in the next breath he told me he wasn't going to talk to her any more. When I asked why he said because she was silly."

"Hmmm, sounds suspicious to me."

"I know. I think he doesn't want to talk to her because I know she exists now. I have been looking at the cell phone bill and there are a lot of phone calls late at night and while he is at his part-time job."

"Something ain't right."

"I know. I just didn't want to go through this bullshit again."

"I know one thing I wouldn't be watching another niggas child, especially when he doesn't want to spend time with him."

"That's the hard part. I feel sorry for the kid. He's always asking where's my dad. When's my dad coming home? Doesn't make me feel good at all."

"That ain't right. Speaking of, where is Kenny right now?"

"I told Alvin I needed a break. I was about to go crazy. The boy doesn't want to go out side and play. Claims it's too hot. He rather stay up under me and ask me a hundred and one questions! So I took him to his brother's house this evening. To make matters worse we had another argument about his other illegitimate son."

"About what?"

"He wants me to meet this son. I told him I am not particularly ready to meet this child."

"Really, what's he want you to do? Go over there with him; sit up there with him and baby's mamma?"

"No, He actually thinks that baby's mamma will let him bring the baby over to my house!"

"What, is he crazy? No mamma in her right mind will let a baby go over some other woman's house she don't know."

"I know, and especially since she wants to still be with him."

"Well maybe you guys should take a break."

"Yeah, maybe we should."

I drove home sadden that evening. I thought this relationship was going somewhere. I thought that I could finally trust men again. Lord, is this what I have to look forward to, men cheating, lying and using me. I got a man that has two bastard children, who claims he wants to marry me but only wants to have one child with me.

What kind of shit is that? Why regulate me because of your mistakes. When will I ever have a relationship that is meaningful? When will I have someone in my life that cares and respects me? I climbed into bed that night feeling totally hopeless. I pulled the covers over my head in hopes of shutting out the world. I wanted to make myself disappear. I didn't want to exist. These damn tears started trickling down my face again.

Running late for work the next morning, I notice Alvin dropped some of the kids clothing on the ground the night before. He has been going over and getting his brother's kids as well and they all have been spending the night at my house. I didn't have time to go back in so I called. "Hmmm, went straight to voice mail. I hung up and called right back. It just rang indicating that he got on his phone as soon as I left. Strange. "Why didn't he make his call while I was getting ready for work?"

He finally called me back about mid afternoon. "I called you this morning to let you know the kids clothes were on the front lawn.

"I know. I got your message."

"Why didn't you answer the phone?"

"I was checking my voice mail."

"Hmmm. Ok well I have to go." I hung up hurt because that was obviously a lie.

The next day, while leaving for work, I called his cell phone again. Same scenario. This time I didn't leave a message. When I got to work, I checked the cell bill online. I found several phone numbers that were called as soon as I left the house. This was crazy! Come to think about it he started going out every Sunday. For a man that doesn't drink, why would he need to be in a club and on a Sunday at that? He also started taking appointments after he gets off work. That's 9:00 O'clock at night! I printed off the numbers. I checked next months bill to see if in fact they are business calls or if they are the same number indicating he is calling some chick. The numbers were the same.

I got home that evening totally distracted. I was tinkering around with the computer, bored, not knowing what to do with myself. I sent Kenny outside. I didn't want to be bothered. "What the fuck is this?" Something told me to check the history on my computer. Alvin has been going to Black Planet checking out all sorts of half clothe women. Every page that I looked at had some half-naked black chick with her boobs or ass hanging out. He even has a site set up as if he was living in the ATL.

Angered, I wondered what else I was missing. I started looking through his papers. Found out that the nigga was only making $25,000 a year and told me he was making $36,000. He also told me that he has to pay about $500 in child support starting next month. Judging by his pay stubs he has been paying child support for a long time. He has two disbursements as if he is paying for two kids. Now he told me emphatically that he was not paying child support for Kenny since he has had him for the last five years. I also found the court documents stating that he had to pay $340 for his new son. Anger unknown gripped me. This asshole has been lying to me the entire time!

With hands shaking, I dial Tory's number. "Hey girl what's up?"

"I can't believe this. I can't believe this."

"Girl you're scaring me what's going on?"

"He has lied to me the entire time." I go on to explain what I found.

"Calm down. Let's get some proof of all of this. Did you get his social security number?"

"Yes."

"What about his passwords?"

"No I couldn't get that."

"Look I have a friend who is a computer expert. He can help you find out all of that information." I will email him right now and let him know what's going on. I am sure he will have some suggestions on how to find out the information needed."

By the next afternoon, I had spyware installed on my computer at home. I ordered all of his past cell phone bills and I had Tory's friend finding out if Alvin had two kids or three. I started calling the numbers on the cell phone bill.

"Hallo" A ghetto-sounding heifer answered.

"Yes, this is Jasmine, and I found your number on my boyfriend, Alvin Marsh's cell phone bill. What is the nature of your relationship?"

"What did you say? Alvin and I have been dating for the last 3 weeks. He ain't got no girlfriend. Who the hell you say you were?" Click. That is all I needed to know. I was livid! "Shit," I said to myself. I need to get out of here. Go home. No can't go home. Go somewhere. I need a drink. While checking my emails, I noticed one from Tory's computer guru.

Jasmine, I hope you will be sitting down when you read this. Your boyfriend Alvin has three kids. There is one in Georgia. The mother' name is LaTia Smith. That's not all. He was dishonorably discharged from the Army for sexual misconduct. The misconduct was towards a man. I am sorry to have to be the bearer of bad news. My advice to you is to dump this loser!

I sat there speechless. I couldn't believe this. I sat there staring blankly at my computer screen. Ring. The phone interrupting my thoughts, I answered absent-mindedly. "Hello, this is Jasmine."

"Why the fuck are you going through my cell phone bills calling my customers?"

"Customers? Boquishea said you guys have been dating for the last three weeks. Motherfucker don't ever call me at work to curse me out?"

"I can't believe this shit. You are invading my privacy."

"Really now. When were you going to tell me that you planned to move back to Georgia and be with your other baby's Mommy, LaTia?

Silence.

"And by the way why don't you tell me about your Army experience?

"What are you taking about?"

"You lying motherfucker! Were you the one who took it up the ass?"

"That's it. I am moving out this weekend."

"You can get out today, you punk ass mother-fucker."

Click. I hung up the phone. It was noon. I knew Alvin was on his way to work. I told my boss that I had an emergency and needed to go. I went straight to Home Depot. I bought new locks for my doors. That afternoon with a bottle of Merlot in hand, I changed my locks; crying, cursing and crying some more. I was completely humiliated. Now I am going to have to get an AIDS test. How could I be so stupid?

I went over to Tory's to drown my sorrows even more. I didn't want to be at home when Alvin got there.

Tory was doing her best to cheer me up. It wasn't working. I was feeling like a total loser. "Tory, I should have known he was on the down low. I mean, he was always so super macho and he always harassed his son saying he didn't want him to turn out to be a punk.

"Girl, how could you have known? He was running around here making babies as well so you couldn't have known."

"I know it's logical to think that way but shouldn't my woman's intuition have kicked in?" As I was nursing my bruised ego my cell phone rings. It was Alvin.

"Aren't you going to answer that?"

"No it's Alvin."

"He'll be calling me in a minute." Just as she said that her phone was ringing.

"Hello" she said. "No I haven't seen her. "Really, she changed the locks!" She said with a stifled chuckle.

While she was talking to Alvin, I checked my voice mail messages:

"Jasmine, baby let's talk about this. I think you got some bad information

Please. I love you. Give me a call."

He sounded so broken, but fuck him. He made a complete fool of me! I never want to speak to him again. The next day I put his belongings outside of my door. I called him and left a message telling him that he better come get his stuff, it looks like rain.

I know it was vindictive but I called everyone on the cell phone bill and told them that they may need to get an AIDS test because Alvin was on the DL. Alvin tried calling me after that but I just ignored his calls.

Next, I had his cell phone cut off. No need for us to have joint cell phone accounts. Let him try to call his skank ass hoe now! Punk Ass!

"Tory, I got an idea. That bastard can't get away with what he did to me. I made copies of Alvin's dishonorable discharge, put his photo on it with the caption: "I love to suck dick." I mailed one to his boss. Now I want to paint the town with these flyers. You game?"

"Girl, Hell yeah, these bastards have been getting away with this shit far too long!"

That night we left the house like two thieves in the night. We were dressed from head to toe in black girl power attire. We got to his block. "Good. He's not home." I said.

"Kill the lights." Tory whispers as if someone is up at this time of night.

We get out of the car armed with bright colorful flyers of Alvin's smiling face alerting the world that he is a no good, booty chasing, lying ass negro who just got busted in his raggedy game.

After we ran around like demons, we went back to Tory's place to unwind. "Girl, break out the Merlot. I think we need to mellow out after that shit. What you got to listen to that will calm a sista down?" She put on some Billie Holliday. "No not Billie. I don't want to go back and kill him because I'm damn sure not gonna kill myself. You got some old Erika Badu?"

After that I was at a low point. For three weeks I was in a state of depression. All I did was lie on my couch and cry. I couldn't eat and I couldn't sleep. I was a mess. I thought of all the horrible relationships I had in the past. First Samuel, then Percy and now Alvin. "Lord," I screamed out. "I can't take anymore."

I finally locked him out of my life and out of my mind. I decided to start going back to church. For the entire six months I was dating Alvin I stopped going. Sunday was here. I was excited about getting back to God. I walked into Holy Hope Baptist Church and sat down in the back. The praise and worship session was awesome. I praised God like never before. I was praying for forgiveness. "Lord please forgive me for my fornication. Please forgive me for not staying connected to you and being in your presence on Sunday mornings. In Jesus name, Amen."

No sooner had I sat down, here comes the Marsh family. Alvin was holding the baby he tried so desperately to hide from me, his baby's momma, his momma who he tried to talk me into letting her stay with us, his brother and his brother's kids. All I could think was, is this a joke? I couldn't believe this!

I decided to hold my head up high and be the bigger person. When Pastor Hopewell called for the congregation to meet and greet everyone, I went over to the happy little family to say hello and God bless you. Alvin stood up came out into the aisle and the next thing I heard was "Oh my God, He just hit her" as I was fading to black!

The hospital

I paused for a second. Joy asked "So what did you learn from Sweet Georgia Brown?"

"You know that old saying that all that glitters ain't gold? Well it maybe a cliché but it is so true. Sweet Georgia Brown was all glitter. He said the right things. He made the right promises. He talked the right talk. He never delivered on any of it. Something deep within me told me he was trouble. I didn't listen. I learned that you must trust your intuition. I also learned that you desperately need time in between relationships to heal and discover yourself again. I didn't take the time to do that. I went into this relationship blindly and as a fool." With that I went on with my torture. Some call it purging the soul. But to me I felt tormented. Part of me felt compelled to tell it all and bare my soul but the other part wanted to simply bury it, reinvent myself and never speak of it again.

Militant Mike- Mr. 23

You say you went white because a sista so deeply hurt you

You say you went white because no sista could ever understand you

You say you went white because we sistas deserted you

You say you went white because no sista could ever love you the way you needed to be loved

Your heart is torn apart from the mama that was never there for you and the daddy that left you. You are mad at mama for working two jobs to support you and put you through school.

Your thank you to her is to bring Becky Sue home to validate you and say look mama I've made it cause Becky Sue loves me and sees me as the man I am. Mama shakes her head as if to say I've failed you. You never learned the lesson of community love and loyalty. My hard work is for not because you will dilute and pollute our royal bloodline with this swine that cares nothing for you.

You parade her into our communities and wonder why no one adores and accepts you

You get angry because sistas now ignore you
You cry the rally cry and try to rally the troupes but no one pays attention to you
You hurt because your people turn their back on you
You don't understand this because Becky Sue has your mind twisted and dismantled she tells you her family is the only family you need but they call you nigger too
You come to yourself too late for all and you go home and cry into your mother's arms she tells you she tried to educate you from the beginning that the white man is the devil and hated you. His very plot was to kill you by any means necessary you poor misguided soul now you have to live with the torture and torment for turning your back on your race and the sista who raised you.

Nigger. When I heard that word from a white person, I knew I was different. In my neighborhood, we were all African American so we knew no difference. Yeah we joked and called each other nigga but that was different. My mother thought it would be good to send me to a multicultural school. So in the third grade I went to Westside Elementary on what seemed like the other side of the world to me. I wasn't afraid though. My homeboy Pete, aka Stretch, was with me. He got his name because he always seemed to stretch the truth!

Our first bus ride out of D.C.'s inner city was breathtaking. I never knew how a neighborhood could look without all of the congestion, trash, and graffiti. A sudden sadness took over me. I started to wonder if my family would ever get out of the projects and live in one of these fine houses.

Our bus finally stopped in front of our new school, Stretch looked at me and I looked back with a wide-eyed grin trying to hide my fear. We exited the bus along with all the other little black children from various inner city neighborhoods.

There were cheery blond haired and blue-eyed ladies waiting for us. I thought to myself, where are all the sisters at. These ladies personally escorted us to our perspective classrooms. I was a little disappointed that Stretch and I were not in the same room. I guess I was going to have to be brave and go it alone.

The blond lady dropped me off to my classroom. I was shocked into silence. I had never been in a room in which I was the only black person. So I stood there, part way in the classroom trying to decide if I was going to bolt or sit down. Then out of no-where, this portly red haired boy with ungodly looking freckles all over his face and arms turned and said to me "What's the matter Nigger? Can't you talk and walk at the same time?" My eyes narrowed as I looked at him. You see in my hood them is fighting words. I was about to let him have it but my new teacher came to greet me and escorted me to my seat. She started to introduce me to the class; I didn't have the chance to let that little punk know who he was messing with. I wanted him to know I wasn't afraid of him. I had a distinct feeling that we weren't in Kansas anymore!

As I sat listening to Mike's words in my race relations class, I was mesmerized. He went on to say that he and Stretch were terrorized that school year by the white kids. He stated that he decided to become the best black man that he could be. He was determined to embrace his African heritage and never let anyone deter him or tear down his history and legacy. I could see where he got his nationalism.

Mike Clarkson was the type of brother who was down for his people. I believe if you lift up his shirt you would find hidden a red, green and yellow tattoo of Africa on his back. He was such a serious man to be so young. He was from the heart the D.C. projects. He was the product of a single mother with a deadbeat criminal father. His mother struggled to raise him and his three sisters in the projects. You could tell he loved his mother and had great respect for what she did for him.

He was a sweet outspoken twenty-three year old. He was the intellectual type trying to be hard-core, which he didn't do very well. When I met him I could tell he had a tortured soul. The eyes always told your deep dark secrets. I got the feeling he wanted to be saved. He wanted a sister like me to save him and make his world right. He wanted a real relationship with someone like me. I didn't think much of it but Mike did. I was just nice to him in sort of a big sister kind of way.

It all started with our final papers in the class. Mike did his on inter-racial dating. Why he did this was beyond me. The class had several strong opinionated sisters in there including the liberal white ones. We all were highly vocal and passionate about voicing our opinions as well. Mike thought it best to cut his presentation on his paper short. He didn't want to get into a heated discussion with the women in the class.

He called me later that week claiming to have something on his mind. For the life of me, I didn't have the slightest clue as to what he wanted to discuss with me. I agreed to meet him. Curiosity got the best of me.

We met for coffee. We went to this small quaint coffee shop in the garden district, the artsy part of town. The lighting was soft and alluring. The incense was pungent and intoxicating. Intellectuals were sitting in various corners engaging in soft debate with sisters who looked like they just stepped out of an ad for United Colors of Benetton.

I stopped to take a long look at Mike before we ordered. I never noticed his striking good looks. It could have just been the lighting in there but his light brown eyes were twinkling. He was 6'2" and had a basketball player's physique. He just gazed at me as if he was in the best dream of his life. The thought crossed my mind that this was blatantly erotic. I was wondering if Mr. 23 was trying to seduce me.

He stared intently into my eyes for what seemed to be a long time and in this tentative small voice asked me, "What is your opinion on interracial dating?" That was a strange question to ask I thought; setting all sorts of bells off in my mind. I looked into his soft baby brown eyes contemplating whether or not to tell him raw and real or should I soften the blow. I chose the soft route. I kept telling myself that he was only twenty-three.

I responded with "I feel that if a man truly loves the white woman then by all means follow your heart. But if he is doing it because he feels black women are inadequate in some way then I don't agree with it. I feel the person really needs to examine why he or she is dating out of their race to see if there are hidden ugly feelings they are trying to forget or erase."

"What if they just truly love each other, do you feel the person is betraying their race?" He asked.

"You are talking about two different issues. If nationalism and being a defender of your race is your life's purpose then yes I feel he or she would be a trader. If the person is just a regular Joe Blow going through life and just happened to fall in love with someone of another race then no I don't believe he is betraying his race." I responded.

Mike gets this sullen look on his face. He seemed as though he was in another place trying to work out something in his mind. His face scrunches up. He shrugs his shoulder. He then changes the subject.

"So why are you single?" He asks me

"It's by choice." I retort.

"That's not telling me anything. You mean someone as fine and as intelligent as you are chooses to be alone? Who hurt you?"

"What makes you think someone hurt me? Why can't it just be I want to be alone to enjoy being with me? I am on a journey to discover self. What's wrong with that?"

"That's bullshit!"

"Why is it bullshit?"

"Because no woman chooses to be alone."

"Why do you think that?"

"No one wants to be alone and lonely."

"Who says I am alone and besides alone and lonely are two different things. Which one are you talking about?"

"Well loneliness, I guess."

"I am not lonely. I love my life. I am living my best life ever."

"Really?" He said half asking half-unbelieving.

"How so?" He asked

"I am basically calling all the shots and not letting a man do it for me. I am making my own decisions. I am taking chances that I would have never taken in the past. I've been enjoying things that I would have never dreamed of trying."

"Hmm it seems as though you are living for you now. That's good. So tell me what happened that led you on this journey of self discovery."

We banter back and forth like that for about an hour or so. I ended up telling him about my failed marriage and my horrible relationship with Percy. I told him about Alvin. I also told him that I was happily single despite all of my mishaps in love.

He apologized to me for all of the men who hurt me. He said he felt bad being a black man representing a race of men who hurt black women. I was thinking this young man would be a good husband to some young black woman one day.

We talked in dept of the plight of black relationships. We put our heads together to try to come up with an answer to the age-old problem of how to keep black love strong. It was nice just vibing like this. He was pretty insightful to be so young.

"Since you are being so forthcoming and truthful tell me what you really think about interracial dating?"

"I told you already."

"You told me the watered down version. Something tells me that you are very passionate about this subject."

"The only thing I really hate about it is the fact that these brothers always blame the sisters for their failures in black on black relationships. It is always are fault they aren't mature enough or man enough to handle a relationship with us. They are always claiming we are bitter, loud talking, lazy, fat, ignorant and what ever else.

It makes me mad they don't respect us, treat us like dirt and treat them like queens. They build homes for them, create families with them, and do nothing for us because they feel we're gold diggers. What is so wrong with wanting to have nice things and a husband capable of providing them? It hurts to be treated like dirt when you do nothing but support the black man and they thank you by turning their back on you."

"I don't think they intentionally do that. I believe in total equality and if you love someone from another race then you should be allowed to without all the back lash."

"So demanding respect is back lash?"

"No but a lot of brothers get much grief from sisters when they are with their white woman. In my opinion there shouldn't be racial tension in the first place. We should all just get along."

"Now we all know that will not be the case in this United States, where everything is based on the color of your skin. Besides, how would you feel if you are constantly put down and told members of another race are better than you? It doesn't feel good. It doesn't feel good to be alone because your man is out with a white woman all because he feels she validates him!"

"I guess you got a point." Mike said conceding.

It seemed to get dimmer in here as the evening slowly crept on. Mike moved in closer and grabbed my hand. I felt as if I was intoxicated but all I had been drinking was coffee. "So Ms. Jasmine what are you looking for in a man?" He whispered seductively.

"Well, I can tell you what I don't want."

"Ok, that's fair."

"I don't want a man who has forgotten all of his dreams. He has to have a purpose to his life. He has to pursue his life's calling. He has to be secure in himself and not look to me to validate him. He can't be controlling, selfish and egotistical. He needs to be sensitive but not a wimp. He has to be strong without being dominant. He has to be fun loving but not a buffoon. He can't be a player. He needs to be a one-woman man. See, I don't want much." I said with a laugh.

"No you don't. What you are asking for seems reasonable."

"Well then why do black men look at me as if I'm asking for their left kidney?"

"I don't know sweetie. Maybe they were not real men."

"Maybe so. That is why I am single now. Don't want to put up with the bull shit."

"Maybe you should try a young man."

"Been there done that twice as a matter of fact. Don't want to go there again. A lot of them are immature."

"Not all young men are immature. I'm not."

"So Mr. Clarkson, are you campaigning for my hand?"

"No." he said rather abruptly.

"Oh, I was just kidding. I didn't mean to offend you."

"No you didn't offend me. You just took me by surprise with that question. It was quite forward."

"So that makes me think the thought of you and I crossed your mind."

Looking very startled I dared to ask that question, I could tell he was weighing his answer very carefully.

What he said to me melted my heart. "Yes from the day I laid eyes on you I felt you were a woman I had to meet. You were sophisticated, beautiful and regal. You are a queen who deserves the best in men; a king who knows how to finesse and caress you like no other. Jasmine, I can tell by looking deeply into your beautiful light brown eyes that men you truly loved have hurt you. I long to change that for you. I long to erase the hurt and replace it with peace, love and tranquility. I just couldn't rest until I was welcomed into your presence in hopes of making your life better."

"Wow, I don't know what to say to that. My heart tells me you could be sincere but my mind tells me it's impossible for you to have those deep feelings for me so quickly." I continued to look into his soft sincere eyes, searching for the clues. I wanted to know if he was kicking me some bullshit. I saw no traces. Could it be that my heart could be mended and my negative opinion of the black male species could be erased all at the hands of Mr. 23? Who is his young black militant brother who is so down for his people, who's so idealistic, who's so passionate about making a change. He was intriguing me.

He was making feel black on black love was making a comeback. He was making me feel that I too can have a black man love me. He was making feel like anything was possible.

"Well I do." He said after a pregnant pause. "I know you don't believe that but it's true. Come on now didn't you tell me you were a hopeless romantic? Don't you believe in love at first sight?"

"Well it is true I am a hopeless romantic but who's lost her belief in the black man. I must say though, you are single-handedly restoring my faith." I said blushing like a schoolgirl. He looked a little dejected when I said that. I couldn't imagine why.

"Before you put your total faith in me", he stated slowly, "I have something to tell you."

"Ok." I said starting to get a little worried. I was thinking is he going to tell me he's dying or something.

"I'm ah I'm engaged."

"What!"

"Hold on wait, wait let me explain. I am engaged but we are taking a break."

"But you are still engaged."

"I know but I'm not sure I want to marry her."

"Why, what's wrong with her?"

"Nothings wrong with her. I'm just not sure that she is the one for me."

"Really now, so what's the issue then?"

"Well, you remember the topic of my paper?"

"Yes all too well."

"Well, um, she's white."

"I see." I said trying to hide my shock and disappointment. How can a man so militant and so pro-black contemplate marrying a white woman? "Why are you involved with a white woman, if I may ask?"

"I went to undergrad with predominately white people. There were no quality women of color at my school. If there were more women like you then maybe I would have chosen differently."

"I see." I said a little annoyed now. Didn't we just talk about that? Didn't I just tell him that it upsets me to hear black men say that? What the fuck if a black woman is in college then that is quality period. I know he knows how hard it is for us to go to college in the first place.

"So describe to me what types of black women were there."

"Well it's hard to explain. The ones I liked didn't like me. They wanted to play the field. They were just not sophisticated, put together, and I hated the fact that they had fake hair."

"I see." I responded trying to keep my temper in tact.

"Can you say something more then I see?"

"What else do you want me to say? You are sitting her telling me how pro-black you are and how you want to go back to the heart of DC's hood to help your people and you're contemplating marry a white woman! What you gonna do take your white queen, plop her down in the middle of the hood and expect to be accepted? Hell what makes you think she wants to go?"

"She does. She's a school teacher and she request to work in a diverse school here!" He said getting a little huffy with me.

"Working an Omaha inner city school is different then working in a DC inner city school. Besides I guarantee she will have your ass in the suburbs so quick before you could complete the last verse of "We Should Overcome." Call me in about ten years after you have your half-breed babies, living in the suburbs, and dining with the Vanderbilt's. Then talk to me about black power and black unity."

"Damn why so much hostility?

"You are sitting here trying to hit on me. Asking me, in so many words, to save your sorry ass and you are engaged to a white woman. How do you want me to react? You are young and naive to think you will be able to parade your white woman around in the hood and think it'll be fine!"

"I thought coming to you and letting you know you are the type of woman a man like me is looking for would be flattering. I am not trying to be saved. I may be a little lost at the moment but I am certainly not looking to you to save me."

"Then what are you trying to do? If you are as confused about the relationship now then why are you getting married? It's not going to get any easier."

"We are just taking a break. I am not confused."

"Oh so you figured you would sew your wild oats with me and go back to your white queen."

"No, that's not it. I was looking for a reason to date black women again. I guess with this type of attitude I chose the right woman."

"Really now, does your white queen know you were trying to get into my drawers? I didn't come seeking you out. You came after me. Oh my bad, just fuck the black woman and marry the white one! Fuck you. I'm out!" I got up and left with such furry and quickness that Mike didn't have a chance to rebut.

I was heated. Driving home I tried to figure out why I was so angry. I guess I was very offended at the fact he would dare come on to me and then tell me he was engaged, regardless of if they were taking a break or not! I was angry at the little respect he gave the sisters at his school. I am sure they were fine he just wasn't into them. How dare he try to use me to save him to redeem himself? Who did he think I was? I was angry for every black woman who was dissed by a brother seeking white women. I was angry for each one of my married friends who found out their husbands were cheating on them with a white woman. I was angry for all of our mother's pains behind the cruelty of a black man. I was angry at the entire black male population for putting the black woman through agony since the dawn of time. I was angry at myself for the twenty-one years I spent on loving black men only to have them not love me back. I was angry at black men for claiming to love me but could not because they did not love themselves. It hurt to come to the realization that I may never have a functioning relationship with a black man.

And as always I cried.

The Hospital

"Joy" I whispered. She was looking at me intently.

"Yes" She said softly.

"What are you thinking about?" I asked. I didn't want to think about me any more. The dreams were getting worse. I had an evil foreboding that I did something so heinous that my mind was hiding it from me.

"I was thinking about the first time Tommy made love to me." She said in a hushed whisper as if by letting that out she would be taken a way from here in chains.

"What but wasn't he your teacher, your protector?" I said.

"Yes." She paused.

"And, what happened?"

"I became his ward. He found good homes for my middle brothers and sister's but the baby stayed with us." She shuddered. I could tell a sudden chill went up her spin as she remembered. "I missed my brother's and sisters terribly. I was feeling real lonely. I held my baby sister close to me every night. I couldn't even believe my mother. I couldn't believe she just up and left us. The family I worked so hard to keep together was scattered."

"I know that had to cause you a lot of pain." I whispered.

"He would come in and comfort me at night. I didn't think nothing of it. I just thought he was being fatherly."

Joy

"Don't cry Joy. It's not so bad here is it?" Tommy said.

"I just miss them so much. I feel lost and lonely. I just, I just want my Mommy." He just hugged me tight. I just let him hold and caress me. I clung to him for dear life.

"It's going to be all right." Tommy cooed again. His hands were rubbing my inner thighs just inches from my female center. When he got close he stopped himself. He got up. I could tell he was aroused. I didn't want to think about that. All I wanted was to feel safe and loved. I wanted a real family, just someone to love me.

For a few months my baby sister and I lived like queens. What ever we wanted or needed Tommy provided them for us. I was starting to feel safe, so I let my guard down.

"I fixed up the room down the hall for your little sister." Tommy announced out of the blue one day.

"Why, she's just a baby. She can stay in here with me." I said desperately. I didn't want her taken away from me too.

"She's four going on five. You just turned thirteen. Don't you want your own room for some privacy?"

"No. We're fine. Thank you." I said as if I was the final authority.

Tommy stared at me. That look sent chills up my spine. He looked so evil. I shuddered. He finally stated that my little sister would be moving into her own room that evening and that was final.

"Shhh sissy I will just be down the hall." Her crying broke my heart even more. "I'm not going any where. I will be here when you wake up." She kept crying. I had to rock her to sleep. Tommy was in the background yelling for her to shut up. I wanted to cry myself. I put my hands over my ears for just a minute. I had to do something so I prayed. I wasn't the praying kind but I just felt something evil hovering.

Baby sister finally went to sleep. I was so afraid to go back to my room. I didn't know why though. Tommy was so good to me. I finally snuck out of my sister's room. I tip toed down the hall. I noticed Tommy's bedroom door was closed. I sighed with relief. I slowly opened my bedroom door. I didn't want to wake him. When I got my door open, I stopped suddenly my eyes bugging out of my head. I couldn't believe what I was seeing. Tommy was lying in my bed naked stroking himself.

"Come in baby." He said in a hushed whisper. Visions of what Drisco did to me flashed through my head. As I got closer he saw my eyes wide with fear. He stopped stroking him self and pulled the covers over me. "Baby I'm not going to hurt you. Come get in bed with Daddy. I will never hurt my baby."

I climbed in bed. I was shaking; terrified that he would rape me. He didn't though. He just held me close, gently stroking my hair. From that point on, he spent the better part of the year assuring me that I was safe with him. I couldn't ask for more. He was a perfect gentleman. He still slept with me though. Sometimes I would wake up to him masturbating.

That entire time he never touched me. He did special things for me. One time we went into the city for a shopping spree just for me. I was so amazed. I never really had new clothes before. I felt like a princess. He let me pick out what ever I wanted. I was always conscious though. I didn't want to spend too much money cause I didn't want to wake up again and have no home and no food to eat.

Funny back then I was always afraid of being left to fend for myself and my sisters and brothers. I was always on the edge. I always felt that anxiety, never safe. Tommy made me feel safe. He comforted me when I cried myself to sleep at night. He praised me when I did well in school. I never had a man in my life that cared for me. I never knew my real father so he became my father.

I really believed he loved me. He kissed me on the lips all the time. I just thought that was normal even though deep down it really didn't feel right. I remember the day when I fell in love with my father.

Tommy was so careful of my feelings. He would ask me if I was ok like constantly. He would ask my opinion on things. Nothing really important, just stuff like what I wanted for dinner or what color I thought the kitchen should be painted. That made me feel like I was important, important to him.

He let me take care of all the household stuff. He depended on me to wash his clothes, cook and keep the house clean. After a long day at work he would come home and confide in me. I started to feel like his equal. I started to feel grown up. He trusted me enough to confide in me real personal things because of this I felt that he actually loved me. That was something I never felt before, not even mother's love. Somewhere in all those late night talks completely nude he made me his wife. No we really never took vows but we shared everything as though we were married.

One night after an extremely hard day, Tommy came into my bedroom. It was strange. He had pajamas on. He never wore those. He also had tears at brim of his eyes just waiting to spill. I was scared.

"What's wrong Tommy?" I said. My voice was shaking with every word I uttered.

"Babe, Just a really bad day. I don't want to worry you with it. I'm just going to sleep in my room tonight."

"But you always sleep in here." I whined, forgetting my newfound maturity. I was feeling abandoned again.

"I know sweetheart but I got to go." As he was saying this a lone tear slid down his cheek.

Tommy left thinking he couldn't do this to another child but he just couldn't help himself. Because of his appetite for young girls he was forced out of the Chicago school system to God forsaken Alabama. He was just lucky they didn't put anything on his record.

He quietly closed his bedroom door, half hoping that Joy would just disappear and half-hoping she would come to him on her own accord. He reasoned that way at least he could say he never forced her. The problem with Joy is that he really loved her. He never wanted to hurt her but he couldn't go without sex another year.

As that thought slid through his mind, Joy slowly opened the door to his room. She walked in timidly. She was so alluring when she was timid, Tommy thought.

"Tommy?" she said in this hushed whisper.

"Yes." I said my voice straining and my manhood stiffening.

"I'm just worried about you? Can I get in the bed with you?" She said with that southern drawl I loved so much.

"Yes come on." I said with much anticipation. I pulled the covers back slowly. She climbed in. She looked deeply into my eyes. I forgot in that moment she was a child. I slowly lifted her gown over her head. She didn't stop me. She lifted my tee shirt over mine. I didn't stop her. We got all of our clothes off. We were completely naked, completely vulnerable. She touched my tear stained cheek. I kissed her hand. We made love. We were two wounded animals trying to console each other and wash away all the pain that in all actuality was the catalyst that brought us together.

"I love you." Joy whispered in my ear.

"I love you too." I said and meant it this time.

Hospital

With that said, Joy was spent. She turned her back to me. I knew she was crying. I could totally understand her pain. I know how it was to love someone so deeply even though it was a lie, even though you knew deep down in your heart it was wrong in every since of the word.

Music Man

After being out in the dating scene for a while, I came up with several categories for the fools I became acquainted with. The first category of course is maintenance man. That's where a guy is cute, body's got it going on and most importantly, he services you when you so desperately need it. Hence, the maintenance man, the only thing he's good for is a good lay.

The second category is Datable. This is the kind of brotha' that has it going on all the way around. He's secure in self. He's stable meaning he won't be hitting me up for a loan. "Sista can I hold a twenty spot." That works my everlasting nerves. He's educated and he knows what a date is. Not the let's go to Micky D's and grab a burger. He knows where to take a lady.

Then there is the Friend. He's the kind of guy that has it all together but for some odd reason you just can't get with it. He's got something missing like an important screw that if he doesn't have it tightened then the brotha' is straight crazy. He's also the nice guy that your mommy always wants you to date but you don't want to because you know he belongs in the nut house and he will eventually get there one day.

This next category we as women know all too well. This is the Busta category. You know the type. The one's who think they are in fashion because their shoes match their shirt, their powder blue shirt with the matching powder blue slacks and Kangol. He's cocky but thinks he's confident. He's ignorant but thinks he's intelligent, and plain irritating to be around.

The last category is my favorite category, the Punk Ass category. This is the brotha' who is the trickster. He's the one who starts out in the datable category. You get a little crazy about him. He has the degrees. He has the conversation. He knows how to dress in every situation. He knows what a true date is. So you think. After four to six months of bliss together the real Punk Ass comes out. He tells you that he has a six month old child or that he's a cross dresser or that he's really broke and can he borrow $3,000 before they put him in jail. You know the type. They come up with some off the wall bullshit that totally takes you for a loop that you just weren't expecting.

This makes me think of Music Man aka Leo Avery. He went from datable to punk ass in zero to sixty seconds. He was what you would call a "nice" guy, the one your mother always tells you to date. They are the ones that don't look like much but they will treat you well. They won't lie to you. They are supposed to worship you and treat you like a queen. Well I tried a nice guy. I was open minded and willing to change my criteria and give the quote unquote "nice guys" a chance. I was totally disappointed.

I met Leo Avery online. Yes, I admit it. I was desperate and lonely so I thought I'll give it a try. I know, what a doofus thing to do but Mr. Avery seemed safe. He was cute and he was in my hometown so I initiated contact with him. We were to meet at a neutral place so I chose a coffee shop. I figured that way, if he was a total goofball, I could drink one cup of coffee and be out.

The day was finally here and I was a little anxious. I got to the coffee shop. I was worried because I was a little late. He wasn't there. I panicked. I didn't have his phone number with me. I sat there looking around trying to remember the number. While pulling out my phone to check to see if his number was still in there, it rang.

"Hello"

"Hey Jasmine this is Leo. Were we supposed to meet at the Village Inn?" He said in this nasally voice I was just now noticing all the while thinking Panera and Village Inn don't sound anything alike.

"No" I said sounding a bit confused. "We were supposed to meet at Panera. Are you at Village Inn?"

"Why, yes I am." He said sounding nerdier by the minute and irritating the hell out of me. "I'm so embarrassed. I'm so sorry." He rambled on.

"Don't worry about it I will come over there."

I got in my car to head across the street. A little frustrated. There he was, this milk chocolate brother with glasses. He looked nothing like his picture. He was dressed in an oversized pale green Army coat. I call them serial killer coats. He had on some faded jeans, not the ones that were in fashion. They were worn and faded because he bought them in 1983 and was still wearing them. He also had on a black stocking cap, the ones serial killers wear in all the movies. Oh Shit. I said to myself. What in the hell did I get myself into? Thank God we are in a public place and we drove separately!

We sat down to breakfast. Although it was supposed to be just coffee, he offered to buy breakfast so I said what the hell; I am here, might as well eat. We got to chit chatting about the usual: where you were from, what you did, and family background. He then got to telling me about his nieces and how he was helping them with their homework the last time he was home. What a bizarre man, I thought.

"Jasmine, so do you know what the definition of a light year is?" Leo asks in the midst of telling me about his nieces back home in Seattle.

"No, I can't say as I do." He tells me the definition and I know he can read the expression on my face because I have this uncanny ability to tell you to fuck off all in one facial expression. I had this look on my face of who the hell cares. Then I remember that I am on a first date and so far serial killer is somewhat nice so let me smile.

I put on my fake smile and say, "thank you so much for enlightening me. I never knew what the definition of a light year was." And I'll be damned he kept pushing the issue.

"Jasmine now you know what the definition of a light-year is. If someone should ask you, you will be able to tell them. Isn't that great?" He says.

I'm thinking to myself, now I will not be on "Who Wants to be a Millionaire" anytime soon, so who the hell is going to ask me what the definition of a light-year is. I was thinking to myself this man is crazy. No wait Jasmine. You want a nice guy. You've been looking for an intelligent guy, give him a chance. I plaster my fake smile on my face once again and changed the subject to the upcoming New Years Eve.

He told me that he didn't have a date and would I like to spend it with him. I hesitated. I didn't know him from Adam and New Years Eve was in two days. I finally told him that I will think about it and get back with him. We continued our breakfast. I found out he was a musician who has perfect pitch and that not many musicians had this perfect pitch. I also found out he never finished college. He was from Seattle and he moved here with the military. He was a twin and he loved his mommy. Lord, what have I gotten myself into?

I left that morning very confused. I really didn't like him but everyone was pushing me to date someone "nice". I couldn't shake the feeling that something wasn't quite right about this man. He seemed sort of off. I ignored my instincts and went ahead and had another date with him. I didn't go out with him on New Year's

Eve. I felt that was too personal. That was a time to spend with someone you really love.

I went out with him about a week later. He had a gig he was playing at one of the local Caucasian bars. He invited me to come see him play. He was a keyboard player. It was a nice night until I got up to go to the bathroom. When I got back, two white women were sitting at our table talking to Leo. One of the ladies was in my seat. When I walked up to the table, Leo introduced us but the woman would not move over and get out my seat. I was heated. What really pissed me off was the fact that it was just plain rude. I know if I saw three empty chairs one with a drink in front of it I would sit in a chair that didn't have a drink in front of it! It's not rocket science. I reached over her, still standing to grab my drink to take a sip.

"Oh, is this your seat?"

Barbie aka White Bimbo who thinks her shit don't stink, thinks she is better than everyone and the world owes her something; said to me. I gave her the *yeah bitch* look, smiled and as politely and sarcastically as possible said, "Yes that's my seat."

She reluctantly moves her white ass over but kept talking and didn't include me in the conversation! To make matters worse another white Barbie spilled her drink on me while passing by and Leo's breath stank!

I made it an early night. I drove home in a funk. I called Tory. "Tory, girl you wouldn't believe the joker I went out with tonight!"

"Girl was it music man!"

"Yes, and he was in rare form. We went to this bar off 164th and Q Street."

"Um the white part of town."

"Yeah girl. There was only a few of us in there." I went on to tell her my experiences with the Barbies. She hated Barbies more than I did.

"Girl you know them stank ass bitches think they own the world and you need to jump for they asses!" I finished telling her about my magical date and I had her cracking up.

I went to bed that night sad. I was trying to recoup from several bad relationships. My relationship with Samuel was bad. My relationship with Percy was really bad. My relationship with Alvin made me angry and now here's Leo the nerd.

I still didn't heed my inner voice. I went out with him again. We just ran some errands like a normal couple and went to dinner. It was nice doing that on a Saturday afternoon. Because I missed that I thought to myself, he's not so bad.

I granted him another date. He invited me to his house. We had a nice time. We watched the "Kings of Comedy."

"Here's some wine for you. I remember you liked Riesling right?"

"Yes," I said with a smile. I was feeling special. It was nice to have dinner and wine waiting for me. Oops I spoke to soon. The brother handed me some wine in a cup. Who drinks wine from a cup? What kind of grown man over thirty-five doesn't have wine glasses!

The evening was nice. It was comfortable or maybe I was just missing the company of a man. Our next date was at his house again. We had lots of wine in a cup. Then he gave me a pedicure. I was so turned on. Not by him but the fact that someone wanted to spend time with me, have dinner waiting for me and give me a pedicure without asking for anything in return. So what is a girl to do? The conversation was nice. He was intelligent. He was making his own money.

The next logical progression was to test the merchandise. Leo turns off the lights and goes into the other room and turns on some soft music. He comes back into the room and undresses me. He gets undressed. My heart starts to race with anticipation. I just knew this was going to be good with all the ambiance and mood setting. And then it happens. He slides himself into me, so I think. He is just humping away and I'm like what is he doing. He was getting all into it and all I can think of was, am I missing something. I couldn't feel a thing. He was going at it, too. He tired himself out and he was making me exhausted just watching this mess. When he was finished and pulled out, I had to look. Low and behold, the man had a four inch dick and that's four inches erect!

I spent a long, horrible night. I didn't want to be rude and get up and leave so I laid their agonizing all night and praying that he would not touch me again. I couldn't bare it.

Finally, it was morning. As I was getting ready to get my clothes and run like a bat out of hell, Leo told me he had a surprise for me. Damn, I thought. Please don't want to have sex again. His new nickname became mini dick.

"Jasmine, I have a surprise for you. Just stay in bed and relax." He said excitedly. He closed the door and disappeared. Thirty minutes later he came back with a tray of assorted breakfast food. I felt kind of bad for my previous thoughts of flight. He fixed scrambled eggs, sausage and cereal. It was way too much. As I began to eat, I discovered the eggs were runny, the sausage was under-cooked and I didn't like the skim milk in my cereal. I know I am being a bitch but damn the brotha can't screw and he can't cook either! How in the hell do you mess up breakfast food!?

I was polite I ate what I could and then I told him I had an appointment that I needed to go home to get ready for. I was moving so quickly that I almost forgot my coat and it was freezing outside.

Once at home, I started to feel bad. He was very sweet and caring. He has done more for me in the short time I knew him then other men I have dated. I decided to call him.

"Leo", he answered my call on the first ring.

"Hey Jasmine. How are you doing? Did you leave something at my house?"

"No, I just wanted to thank you again for yesterday and breakfast this morning. It was really sweet." I responded with softness in my voice.

"Oh," he crooned, "you deserved it. I was glad to do it."

"Well thanks again. I have to go to get ready for my appointment." Had to keep up the pretense no reason to let him know I lied.

"Ok, well when will I see you again?"

"Well just give me a call later on in the week and we can set something up." I still couldn't get over his childlike dick.

"Ok I will do that. Have a good day." He said in his nasally voice. "Ok Jasmine be nice." He is trying hard here.

"Cool and I will." I said trying not to sound irritated.

I invited Leo to my house for dinner for our next date. I felt that he was taking me out and spending money on me the least I could do was fix the brother a meal. He came over with his same old goofy self. He had on his signature faded jeans, a sweater, and his green army coat with black stocking cap. What a nerd I thought!

We ate dinner. He didn't appear to like my cooking. That pissed me off especially since he kept saying everything was good and he only ate a portion of his food. We adjourned to the couch. "Damn," I said to myself. He wanted a kiss and damn his breath stank! I did the avoidance dance all night. We ended up falling asleep on the couch watching DVD's. I so wanted him to go home. He was irritating me. I woke up first. I started cleaning up. I went back into the living room and Leo was waking up.

"Hey Jasmine, thanks for dinner again."

"You're welcome. I'll go get your coat." I went to grab his coat and handed it to him. He looked dejected. I didn't care though. I wanted him out of my house. I suddenly became very tired and angry.

"Are you missing anything?" I said totally irritated.

"No." He gets up, starts slowly putting on his coat and his stalker's ski cap. *He's just pissing me off. Taking his time and shit. It doesn't take that long to put on a coat. Damn, hurry up! Keep cool. Don't get angry. He's almost out the door.* I said to myself. As we were at the door Leo turns back to me and whined, "But I want to stay."

Totally exasperated I said, "No, you have to go home." I gently pushed him out the door and slammed and locked it quickly. I went to bed. I was spent. I don't know what it was but he really irritated me. I think it was the fact that he really wasn't my type. I liked him but felt pressured into creating this semblance of a relationship because it was socially correct or that he would be acceptable because he was a nice guy. I wasn't tired any more. I was angry. Why? I don't know.

I purposely avoided his calls for the next three days. In that time span he left me umpteen messages. The last one was most disturbing.

Jasmine, I really need to talk to you. It's urgent. Give me a call as soon as you get this message. Ok, I hope to talk to you soon.

When I heard that message I thought something was terribly wrong. I called back right away.

"Leo? Is everything ok?" I asked as soon as he picked up the phone on the first ring.

"Jasmine, hi. Yes everything is fine." He replied.

"Well your message said it was urgent so I thought something was wrong."

"Well no it's just that I really need to talk to you."

"Oh, well what's up?"

"Well, I want to talk to you face to face."

"It sounds serious."

"Well, yes it is."

"Ok when do you want to meet?"

"Tonight if possible."

"Well, tonight I have a commitment, how about tomorrow evening after my class?"

"Ok, that will work. Where do you want to meet? Do you just want to come over my house?"

"No let's just meet at the bookstore, since I will be right over there."

"Cool, I'll see you about 8:30 at the bookstore." After we hung up I got this eerie feeling. What in the world did this man want to talk to me about that was so urgent and that it had to be face to face?

D-day finally came. I got to the bookstore before he did. I sat near the coffee area and started my homework. About twenty minutes later Leo strolls in.

"Hey, Jasmine" He says. "Can we move to a more private area?"

"Sure" I said with my plastic smile on my face a little irritated that I have to shut down my computer and move. We moved to this obscure corner of the book store.

"Well Leo, What's on your mind?" I said wanting to get this over with because I was tired, hungry and wanted to go home.

"Well, um I wanted to ask you, how do you think we are doing?" he said in his nasally tentative voice.

"I guess fine." I replied. I was not sure where this conversation was heading and I wasn't sure I was going to like it once he got to the point.

"Well do you see a future with me?"

"Hmmm, why are you asking all of these questions? Please tell me what this is all about."

"Well, um, I have this opportunity to be in a committed relationship. There's this girl that wants to commit to me and I wanted to see where this was going before I get back to her with an answer."

I didn't know how to take that. I didn't know how he had the time to develop another relationship when he was hounding me all the time. I had to buy some time to think about where he was heading with all of this mess. Something just wasn't adding up.

"So when did you have time to date someone else?"

"Well she's a friend of a friend and she told my friend she wanted to get together with me."

"Oh" I said. That statement confirmed that something in the water just wasn't right. "So, she told you she wants a committed relationship with you?"

"Yes, in so many words, yes."

"She actually stated she wanted to be with you and you have not really dated this woman?

"Ah, yes. Like I said she is a friend of a mutual friend of mine."

"Well in that case I would say go for it. As I told you in the beginning, I am not looking for a committed relationship at the moment. I have too much on my plate. I cannot possibly take on anything else." I replied matter-of-factly. He looked shocked and rejected when I said this.

"Well I just thought that if I had a chance with you then I wouldn't even entertain the thought of getting with this other girl. I was just thinking that we had something going and I didn't want to lose that."

"We do have something going. It's called a friendship. And like I said I am in no position to start a relationship at this point in my life. I don't want to be in the way of your happiness, so, by all means if this girl wants to give you the committed relationship you desire then go for it."

"Ok, you have definitely given me something to think about."

"Hmmm, well is that every thing you wanted to talk about? I am very tired and would like to go home."

"Ok, yes that was it." He replied with a little less steam.

"Ok then I guess I will be heading home." I couldn't wait to call Tory and let her know Music Man just graduated to the Punk Ass category! How dare he try to force my hand? He knows damn well there's no other woman. That's why he can't give me any more detail then he has. He didn't even have his lie straight. What a nerd. I am upset that I even wasted my time.

Two days later I got a call from Leo. He told me he was not going to pursue a relationship with that other girl and how he wanted to continue what we had. I hung up in his face. With the click of the off button on my phone, my brief relationship with a nice guy was over.

From Leo, I learned to follow your heart and never to date anyone because your mother, best friend or sister thinks you should. You should be with someone because you know that person's inner self and you can accept that person for who they are. I have learned one dominating thing about relationships; you cannot change a man. If a man is going to change he will change on his own.

Star Gazer

I should have known better but I was a bit melancholy. I was horny as well. That was a deadly combination; however, I went out with him anyway.

Johnnie Lee Rooker was the kind of guy who lived perpetually in the past. He used to be in a local singing group called the Real Deal or something like that in his early twenties. The man is thirty-seven now and still relates the stories of his hay day as if it were yesterday. He was a trip.

I met him at a reception for Oprah's man, Steadman Graham. The reception was nice. The who's who of Omaha was there. It was held at the Love Music Museum named after the famous jazz musician Preston Love one of Omaha's native sons. The museum was a beautifully refurbished abandoned building on the city's north side. The north side was considered the black part of town also known as the ghetto. It was an elegant affair in spite of its location.

I was dressed in this black, full-length dress with white stitched flowers on the bodice. It fit snugly and hugged my body like an elegantly crafted leather glove. I was practically the only single woman in the room of married men, their wives and mistresses. He was practically the only single man in the room. All eyes were on me. Even the married men were stealing glances at me hoping their spouses didn't catch them looking. I felt good. There's nothing like being the sweet nectar that every king bee craves.

Johnnie Lee Rooker was the acting bartender for the affair. My girlfriend and I went up to get a drink. He was about 5'9", wearing a semi-grey, semi-powder blue suit. I guess you could call the color pewter. He was a dark-skinned brother, the real Hershey chocolate kind. He had a nice faded hair cut. He was clean cut and neat. I liked that. He was not cute by any means but he was charming. He had an infectious personality. He kept making me laugh. Laughter for me right about now was a desperate need.

He was interesting to say the least. He asked me out right on the spot that night. I figured what the hell, if he was bold enough to first of all talk to me and then ask me out, he deserved a chance.

We went to one of the nicer restaurants in town. I was impressed. Dinner was nice. The conversation was great. I laughed. He laughed. It was a relief. I felt no pressure to perform. It was like I knew I was leaving Omaha so this could only lead to two things, good-bye sex or good friendship. The way I was feeling, I hoped it would lead to sex. There's nothing like good sex to send you off in style!

Because we didn't have sex the night we went out, not for a lack of his trying, he continued to call me everyday; making me laugh. It's just like a man, to woo you and woo you until they get the panties and then they forget your name. He was trying really hard. I knew he only wanted one thing but did he know that was all I wanted as well? We made plans to get together the next weekend. I kept going back and forth: should I sleep with him or should I not. I was stressing. I didn't know why though. If I slept with him it would only be a booty call cause in two weeks I was out of Omaha for good!

"Well I guess nobody's hanging out this evening." I finally said to Jamie after we left our third club.

"This is the big O. You know how it is, nothing to do on a Saturday night." He said looking at me intently as he patted my knee.

"Hmm," I said gazing out the window and thinking this is the moment of "I guess we can go back to my place and drink the wine you brought me the other day." I finally said trying to act nonchalant. He gave me that player look. The one that they always give when they knew they were about to get lucky.

We went back to my place. He took my clothes off slowly. We were butt naked. I peered into his eyes. He started to kiss me. I lifted my chin. He kissed my neck. He started to get into it. My mind floated back to every lover I had in my life. I saw every face. I felt every empty emotion. I felt every sadness. I felt every disappointment from each and every one of the men who hurt me.

"Stop," I whispered. It came up softly from my soul. Johnnie ignored me and kept on kissing me.

"Stop," I said again with just a little more force. He hesitated for just a moment. He kept coming after me. I couldn't believe he was trying to force me to have sex with him. He grabbed my arm, gripping it with such force I thought it was going to fall off.

"Stop!" I yelled louder with more force. He stopped and looked at me. I was finally tired of being used. I was finally tired of being taken advantage of.

"Get out!" I yelled at Johnnie. He looked stunned and confused. "Just go. Go home." I walked to the door and opened it wide. He went to the door and suddenly slammed it closed.

"Hell naw!" He yelled at me. "I wined and dined your ass and you ain't giving up the pussy! Hell naw bitch." He grabbed me by my wrists and led me back to the bedroom.

"Get your ass on the bed." I gave him a look of defiance. *Wham.* The fist blow, an open hand, struck me across my left cheek. I gasped.

"You bastard" I yelled.

He hit me again. This time it was a closed fist to the chin. The pain was excruciating. Tears blurred my vision. I couldn't see straight. I looked up suddenly and Samuel was standing over me instead of Johnnie. He grabbed my throat hard. I reached for my knife I kept under my bed. I stabbed him. Trying to remove the vision of him from my site. Percy's face immediately replaced Samuel's. I stabbed again, harder this time. He kicked me in my face. I went back hard against the dresser. I gathered my balance just in time as now Percy was lunging forward upon me trying to kill me. I just kept stabbing trying to kill all of those who hurt me. Stab, kill, stab, kill. That was the mantra that was running through my head. One by one, each of my lovers appeared before me. The hurt they caused me intensified. I kept stabbing until they were all slain.

Tears streaked with blood smeared my face. Suddenly everything went still. Black was all I saw. My mind was whirling out of control. I didn't know what was happening to me. It was too damn quiet. Had to get up. Had to get out. Had to keep moving or else I would die.

The Hospital

I walked away from everything. It was Christmas Eve. I just needed to get to a church. I remembered my mother taking us to mass on Christmas Eve. I knew there was a huge church downtown. If I could just get there. I was in such a daze. I was in a sweat suit and some tennis shoes. I didn't even remember putting that on. All I kept thinking was if I could just get to the church. Beautiful Christmas hymns were playing in my mind. I couldn't hear anything else. The music calmed me. Where's my car? I must have forgotten my keys, forgot to get into my car. I must have wandered around for hours. When I woke up, I was in a hospital bed, confused.

"Tell me who you are? Where you grew up? You seem like such a polished, educated lady. You are pretty, too. Why so much heartache and pain?" Joy asked so innocently. I think she was really trying to find out what happened to me. She was genuinely concerned. It was still hard for me to talk about myself. I didn't want to share my woes with anyone. I guess that's why I liked it here so much. I could bask in my craziness and no one would care. I could have my meltdowns and that would be expected.

"Did you really kill someone?" Joy whispered. I could tell she wanted to purge her soul but she just sat there and waited for my answer.

"I don't know." I said. "I can't remember." I looked away from her, sad at the notion that I actually could have killed someone.

She kept looking at me, expecting me to say something and so I told her the only thing that I was sure of, the amazing story of my childhood. The amazing thing about it was the fact that despite all the heartache and pain I went through, I haven't killed myself yet.

My mother was totally obsessed with my father. She got lost in him. I think that is where I learned it. You know losing my mind over a man. To this day she still loves him. She writes him and tries to call him. He ignores her.

My mother was also a paranoid schizophrenic. All my life she would have these delusions of demons or something that were after her. My sisters and I just thought it was normal. We didn't know any better. But we knew something was wrong, especially since we spent most of our young childhood in foster homes. My mother took care of us the best she could. I don't want to say that I had a bad childhood because it wasn't all that bad. However, while growing up I have always felt my mother hated me. The things she did made me believe she really did.

Mommy, that's what we used to call her; I remember one time all went shopping, my sister's, my mom and I. She told us to each pick out an outfit. We all picked out an outfit that we really liked. I was so excited about this little outfit. You know how little girls do. Their new clothes make them feel like a princess. Well, while my sister's and I were distracted looking at something else, my mother put back what I picked out and got me the ugliest checkered thing she could find and bought it for me. When we got home my grandmother was over and she wanted us to try on our outfits for her.

We ran into the bedroom with the bag to try on our clothes. I was excited because I loved what I picked out. My two sisters pulled out there items and started to try them on. I finally got the bag. I pulled out what was left. I burst into tears running out of the room asking where my clothes were. I was holding up this ugly thing that my mother picked out for me. Tears were streaming down my face. My grandmother swooped me into her arms while asking my mother what she did. My mother just shrugged her shoulders.

The next week my grandmother came over and she had dresses for us. She gave me the most amazing purple dress. I tried it on and felt like a princess. A few hours later I found my dress on our front porch cut to shreds. I ran in crying that my beautiful dress was gone. Come to find out my older sister was jealous and she cut it up. All my mother did was tell her she shouldn't have done that. She didn't even give my sister a spanking. If I would have done something like that, my mother would have beaten me.

I felt that my mother hated me. One time she told me I was ugly. I was just a little girl. Little girls always believe their mothers. I went through most of my adolescence thinking that I was ugly.

"Oh my God" Joy said. "That must have been horrible growing up there."

"Yes it was. That was typical of what happened while growing up. My mother used to let my older sister beat me to a pulp. She let my little sister steal my candy and my toys. Most of the time I played with my dolls. I had several dolls. They were my babies and I loved them all. From the time that I was a little girl I wanted to be a mommy. I wanted to give my child the love that my mother didn't give me. I wanted the type of family that I never had. I wanted the security of love and affection that you should get from your family. I wanted to never be lonely again. I guess that's why I let so many men use me. I needed to feel loved and accepted."

"I know how you feel. I never felt loved, protected or safe at home. I was always afraid. Afraid of everything." Joy said quietly

We sat there silently, just reflecting on our perspective past lives. How hard our lives were. But the operative thing was how hard our lives were. Strangely, I felt that everything would be ok. I had this sneaky suspicion that God put Joy and me together for a reason. I believe God was up to something - hope. It felt good to have it after a long road of heartbreak.

"So what was the single most important lesson you learned from all of this?" Joy asked breaking the silence.

"Well" I said taking a long pause. "The most important thing I've learned was to love God with all of your heart and know and love yourself just as much. You see if you love God and follow him, you will never be lost or lonely. If you love yourself you will never really be crushed when someone doesn't love you back."

"I don't know God." She said. "Maybe if I had, then I wouldn't have done it."

"Done what? I said suddenly really concerned for her.

"Hurt Tommy" She said looking into the distance with this trance-like stare on her face.

"Joy, how did you hurt Tommy?"

"He said he was leaving me. His bags were packed." She said obviously not hearing my question.

"How did you hurt Tommy, Joy?"

"I put something in his coffee. He passed out at the door before he left for work. I didn't think it was going to hurt him, just slow him down. I figured he would be put in the hospital and give him some time to think about what he was doing to me. So, he could see how much I cared for him once he came home from the hospital and I took real good care of him."

"Joy is Tommy all right?"

"I don't know."

"Is he alive?"

"I don't know"

"What happened after he passed out?"

"I went insane. I would love to know him."

"Who Joy?"

"God. Every time my mom would get down she would call on him, or was that Jesus?

"Hey, there's a chapel in this place right?" I said softly. "It's time you meet Jesus. Come on lets go."

"But it's midnight"

"God is always awake."

I grabbed her hand and we snuck out of the room and headed quickly to the chapel. Once we got there we kneeled down. I lead Joy in the Lord's prayer. Joy got saved. I was so happy for her. We walked back to the room arm in arm.

Once Joy was sleeping peacefully, I went back to the chapel. I was anxious and still a little lost. I was still in the nut ward for God sakes!

Hospital

I just realized it was Sunday as I kneeled down at the altar. I told Joy about every heartbreak and all of my lost loves. Telling her these things made me question where I went wrong and how I ended up at this particular fork in the road. I was feeling weak. I questioned why I was still having problems with relationships. I couldn't figure out why I went through hell with all of these men. Panic bubbled up in my soul. I was strong and confident when I was helping other women but when it came to myself I was weak; disoriented. I had to talk to the Lord. I needed answers. Truth be told, I was afraid of what the answers would be. Was I that stupid? Do I hate myself that much? How long was I going to lose myself in a no good man?

Frustration, anger and bitterness crept up my spine. I shook uncontrollably. I kneeled at the alter. I had to purge my soul. I couldn't see through the influx of tears.

Heavenly Father please forgive me for all of my sins. I need you right now, today. I don't know how I got to this point but sometimes I just want to end it all. I don't want to live another day with my heart broken. I am tired of dead end relationships. I am tired of getting stepped on, pushed around and taken advantage of. I am tired of crying a river of tears. You promised me a family and here I am an old maid, alone and abandoned. Why have you forsaken me? Why did I have to go through this bullshit? What is my purpose here on this earth? Why all the pain? Why do they just get to walk off into the sunset and leave me here to pick up the pieces? I am so tired of crying myself to sleep. I am so tired of sleeping alone. I am tired of being treated like a piece of meat or property. When is it going to change? Do you hear me Lord? I am struggling down here?

The tears were streaming down my face. They were coming from deep within. I couldn't stop convulsing. The pain was so deep, so raw. It hurt so much. I felt a tap on my shoulder. I thought it was a nurse trying to usher me back to my room. Looking through my tears, all I could make out was a small blond child with deep blue eyes. The light behind her was too bright. She said, "God hears you and he loves you. He wants you to know, all you need to do is take up his cross and follow him. He wants you to lay every burden at his feet. He wants you to know he will never leave you or forsake you." I cried harder. I looked up again and the little girl was gone. A strange calm came over me. I knew that everything was going to be all right.

I sat there for what seemed like hours reflecting on the role I played in the demise of my relationships. I came to realize that I did not value self. I did not feel I was worthy of love because I did not love myself. I was searching for love in these men only to find the same dejected person in them that I was.

I had a wounded view of love. My first description of love came from my mother who hated herself. She hated her self-image. She wanted to be lighter than she actually was. She hated her body. She tried endlessly to find herself in a string of men. I learned this from her. She also hated me. I really don't know why but I suspect it was because she saw in me what she wanted to be. Her breakdown was the result of not letting go of my father. She could not let that love go. She took his rejection of her out on me. I internalized her hatred of me. Like her, I constantly looked for approval in this mythical perfect man. He did not exist just like a perfect me did not exist.

I internalized all of these things. It engulfed me. I was so naive, thinking if I loved hard and deep then all would work out well. I was wrong. I thought if I improved myself, be the best that I could be, then all would work out. I was wrong. I thought if I forgave and forgot his ill treatment of me then all would work out. I was wrong. No one was there to steer me in the right direction. Every woman I knew was wounded and broken. Every woman I knew had deep scar tissues she was trying to erase to no avail. What kind of world do we live in where our African American brothas don't respect us anymore? Did we come so far over the mountain that we figured we didn't need each other anymore? Why are all the African American women crying and putting masks on their faces to hide their depression? Are we not valuable to our men anymore? I refuse to believe God put us here on earth to hate each other. I refuse to believe that all men are bad.

I place all of this at His feet. I know God loves me. I love me. I know all is not lost. It is all going to work out. I know this because when you go to the brink of insanity and make it through that storm rising like a phoenix, there is no stopping your success.

I went back to my room with a renewed sense of purpose. Calm came over me. I suddenly knew that I was to help other hurting women through the storm. I was to help them make it safely. I knew what the brink of insanity looked like. I knew what it could do to you. I had to help them make it sanely to the other side. I knew that Joy was to help me with this.

"Joy wake up." I whispered a tad bit too loud.

Looking at me sleepily, "what?" she whispered back.

"I feel a little Bonnie and Clydeish."

"What?" she said really confused.

"I really can't explain it all right now but I know we're supposed to work together and help other women like us."

"How we gon' do that, stuck in this nut ward."

"Well what's stopping us from walking out that door right now?"

"Nothing, I guess."

"Come on. Get your stuff and let's blow this joint."

Epilog

Hospital

Ma'am I understand a "Jane Doe" was brought here last week. The officer said to the nurse.

"Yes very odd. She was covered in blood but the only cuts we found on her was her hands. She was pretty beat up though. She was out of her mind. I guess the beating she took also made her lose her memory. She had extensive head wounds".

"I see. Well that's good information. We would like to question her in regards to the death of a young man. If she is who we think she is then she will have a lot of explaining to do. Can we see her?"

"Yes of course. This way, please." The nurse walked somberly to Jasmine's room. She had come to know her in the last week and could not believe she could hurt a fly. She was praying silently for a miracle. The nurse pushed open the door. They stepped into the room. The room was empty. "Well nurse, where is she?"

"Well, I don't know? They were here last night."

"They?"

"Yes, she had a roommate, Joy."

"Well where is Joy? Let's ask her where she is."

"Wait, it looks like all of their personal belongings are gone. Maybe they left the hospital grounds."

"How could this happen?"

"Well we had no reason to hold her she was not committed. She was free to leave when she wanted to."

"What about the other one?"

"Well that's a different story."

"Why are you looking for this girl?" The nurse asked out of fear. She knew Jasmine came to them covered in blood.

"Someone was brutally murdered a few nights ago and from the sounds of it your Jane Doe might fit the description of the person we are looking for."

"Oh my" She was such a lovely girl. Are you sure the person you are looking for is a woman? I mean Jane

Doe was so tiny." The nurse replied trying to cast doubt but deep down she knew her Jane Doe had something to do with the murder from all of the mumbling she did her first night here.

"Yes according to the witness reports. The person we are looking for is definitely female. Did your Jane Doe have any identification on her when she was brought in?"

"No, nothing. Just the clothes on her back."

"Can we see her clothes?" The officer asked.

The nurse got really nervous. She knew if she showed them the clothes, Jane Doe would become their number one suspect. She had a deep feeling that if Jane Doe was involved she had a perfect reason why she killed that person. The wounds on her hands and the bruises on her face showed she was in a battle for her life. "Yes you can see them. I will go get them. I do want you to know the young lady that was brought here was battered and beaten. I believe she was beaten within an inch of her life."

"I see. Well let us make that judgment call. Get the clothes.

The nurse went to gather Jasmine's torn and bloody clothes. Dreading this day would come, she watched the officer examine them with sadness. She grew so fond of Jasmine. She saw how she reached Joy, a feat no one at the hospital could do. She brought light into a place that only had darkness.

"We'll be in touch," the officer said as he hastily left the hospital with the bloody clothes.

www.ingramcontent.com/pod-product-compliance
Lightning Source LLC
Chambersburg PA
CBHW032035150426
43194CB00006B/289